대한민국 영어 구문 학습의 표준

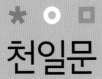

천일문

CEDU(쎄듀)는 **A C**omprehensive **E**nglish e**DU**cation(종합적 영어교육)의 약자입니다.

펴낸이   김기훈 김진희

펴낸곳   ㈜쎄듀/서울시 강남구 논현로 305 (역삼동)

발행일   2021년 10월 18일 제4개정판 1쇄

내용 문의   www.cedubook.com

구입 문의   콘텐츠 마케팅 사업본부
　　　　Tel. 02-6241-2007
　　　　Fax. 02-2058-0209

등록번호   제22-2472호

ISBN   978-89-6806-234-6
　　　　978-89-6806-233-9(세트)

500 SENTENCES
MASTER

천일문 완성

저자

김기훈

現 ㈜쎄듀 대표이사
現 메가스터디 영어영역 대표강사
前 서울특별시 교육청 외국어 교육정책자문위원회 위원
저서 | 천일문 / 천일문 Training Book / 천일문 GRAMMAR
첫단추 BASIC / 어법끝 / 문법의 골든룰 101
어휘끝 / 쎄듀 본영어 / 절대평가 PLAN A / 독해가 된다
The 리딩플레이어 / 빈칸백서 / 오답백서
첫단추 / 파워업 / ALL씀 서술형 / 수능영어 절대유형 / 수능실감 등

쎄듀 영어교육연구센터
쎄듀 영어교육센터는 영어 콘텐츠에 대한 전문지식과 경험을 바탕으로 최고의 교육 콘텐츠를 만들고자 최선의 노력을 다하는 전문가 집단입니다.
오혜정 센터장 · 한예희 책임연구원 · 구민지 전임연구원 · 김진경 전임연구원 · 이누리 연구원

검토에 도움을 주신 분들
안상현 선생님(수원시 권선구) · 조시후 선생님(SI어학원) · 황성현 선생님(서문여자고등학교) · 김명열 선생님(대치명인학원) · 민승규 선생님(민승규영어학원)
안명은 선생님(아우름영어) · 이민지 선생님(세종 마스터영어학원) · 박고은 선생님(스테듀입시학원) · 박혜진 선생님(박혜진영어연구소) · 안미영 선생님(스카이플러스학원)

마케팅	콘텐츠 마케팅 사업본부
영업	문병구
제작	정승호
인디자인 편집	올댓에디팅
디자인	유은아
영문교열	Stephen Daniel White

FOREWORD

천일문 시리즈는 2004년 첫 발간된 이래 지금까지 베스트셀러를 기록하며 전체 시리즈의 누적 판매 부수가 어느덧 430만 부를 훌쩍 넘어섰습니다. 2014년 개정판이 나온 지도 7년이 지나, 쎄듀의 그동안 축적된 모든 역량을 한데 모아 더욱 진화된 내용과 구성으로 새로이 개정판을 내게 되었습니다.

진정한 영어 학습의 출발, 천일문

한문 공부의 입문서인 천자문(千字文)을 배우고 나면 웬만한 한문은 죽죽 읽는다는데, 영문을 공부할 때는 그런 책이 없을까? 천일문(千一文)은 이런 의문에서 출발했습니다. 영문의 기본 원리를 터득하여, 길고 복잡한 문장이 나오더라도 앞에서부터 차례대로 이해하는 올바른 해석 능력을 길러드리고자 하였습니다. 동시에, 삶의 모토로 삼고 싶은, 그래서 저절로 외우고 싶은 생각이 드는 좋은 글로 학습의 즐거움을 드리고자 하였습니다.

문장이 학습의 주가 되는 천일문

천일문은 우리말 설명보다는 문장이 학습의 주가 됩니다. 모든 문장은 원어민들이 실제로 사용하는가(authenticity), 자주 쓸 수 있는 표현인가(real-life usability), 내용이 흥미롭고 참신한 정보나 삶의 지혜를 담고 있는가(educational values)의 기준으로 엄선하여 체계적으로 재구성한 것입니다. 이들 문장을 중요한 구문별로 집중학습할 수 있도록 설계했습니다.

무엇이 개정되었는가

1 문장 교체: 시대 흐름에 맞도록 문장의 참신성을 더하고 최신 기출을 포함시켰습니다.

2 종합학습서: 어법과 영작을 늘려 능동적으로 구문을 적용할 수 있는 기회를 제공함과 동시에, 독해와 내신을 아우르는 종합학습서로의 역할을 할 수 있도록 하였습니다.

3 전략적 구성: 입문-기본-핵심-완성이 기본적으로는 구문과 문장의 난이도가 점차적으로 높아지면서도 각기 고유한 학습 목표를 가지도록 하였습니다. 이는 독해의 기초부터 실전까지 단계별로 학습자들에게 필요한 능력을 효과적으로 기를 수 있도록 한 것입니다.

4 천일비급(별책해설집): 내용을 대폭 보강하여 자기주도적 학습과 복습이 더 수월해졌습니다.

5 학습 부담 경감: 예문의 집중성을 높여, 보다 적은 양으로 학습이 가능하도록 했습니다.

6 천일문 완성 문제집 Training Book: 구문 이해를 정착시키고 적용 훈련을 할 수 있는 충분한 양의 연습 문제를 담았습니다. (별도 판매)

7 무료 부가서비스(www.cedubook.com): 어휘리스트, 어휘테스트, 본문 해석/영작 연습지, MP3 파일, 딕테이션 sheet 등 막강한 부가서비스도 마련하였습니다.

천일문의 새로운 도약을 위해 '대한민국 영어교과서'라는 별칭이 부끄럽지 않도록 1년여간의 연구와 많은 토론으로 최대한의 노력을 기울였습니다. 이 교재와의 만남을 통해 대한민국의 많은 영어 학습자들이 영어를 영어답게 공부할 수 있기를 희망합니다.

저자

SERIES OVERVIEW

기본

입문

기본편이 어려운
학생들에게 권해요.

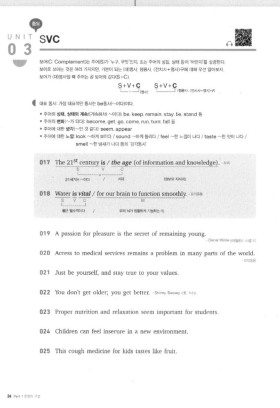

UNIT 03 중요

SVC

보어(C: Complement)는 주어(S)가 '누구, 무엇'인지, 또는 주어의 성질, 상태 등이 '어떤지'를 설명한다.
보어로 쓰이는 것은 여러 가지지만, 기본이 되는 (대)명사, 형용사, 〈전치사+명사〉구에 대해 우선 알아보자.
보어가 (대)명사일 때 주어는 곧 보어와 같다(S=C).

$$S+V+C \qquad S+V+C$$
(명사) (형용사, 〈전치사+명사〉구)

대표 동사: 가장 대표적인 동사는 be동사(~이다)이다.

• 주어의 상태, 상태의 계속(계속해서) ~이다: be, keep, remain, stay, lie, stand 등
• 주어의 변화(~가 되다): become, get, go, come, run, turn, fall 등
• 주어에 대한 생각(~인 것 같다): seem, appear
• 주어에 대한 느낌: look ~하게 보이다 / sound ~하게 들리다 / feel ~한 느낌이 나다 / taste ~한 맛이 나다 /
  smell ~한 냄새가 나다 등의 '감각동사'

017 The 21ˢᵗ century **is** / ***the age*** (of information and knowledge). -모의
    S   V   C
    21세기는 ~이다   /   시대   (정보와 지식의)

018 Water **is** *vital* / for our brain to function smoothly. -모의응용
    S   V   C
    물은 필수적이다   /   우리 뇌가 원활히 기능하는 데.

019 A passion for pleasure is the secret of remaining young. -Oscar Wilde (아일랜드 소설가)

020 Access to medical services remains a problem in many parts of the world. -우리말응용

021 Just be yourself, and stay true to your values.

022 You don't get older; you get better. -Shirley Bassey (英 가수)

023 Proper nutrition and relaxation seem important for students.

024 Children can feel insecure in a new environment.

025 This cough medicine for kids tastes like fruit.

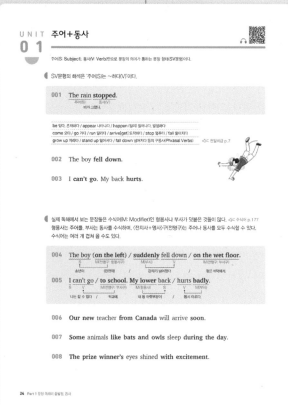

UNIT 01 주어+동사

주어(S: Subject), 동사(V: Verb)만으로 문장의 의미가 통하는 문장 형태SV문형이다.

SV문형의 해석은 '주어(S)는 ~하다(V)'이다.

001 The rain stopped.
    주어(S) 동사(V)
    비가 그쳤다.

be 있다, 존재하다 / appear 나타나다 / happen (일이) 일어나다, 발생하다 /
come 오다 / go 가다 / run 달리다 / arrive[get] 도착하다 / stop 멈추다 / fall 떨어지다 /
grow up 자라다 / stand up 일어서다 / fall down 넘어지다 등의 구동사(Phrasal Verbs) ◁ 천일비급 p.7

002 The boy fell down.

003 I can't go. My back hurts.

실제 독해에서 보는 문장들은 수식어(M: Modifier)인 형용사나 부사가 덧붙은 것들이 많다. ◁ 수식어 p.177
형용사는 주어를, 부사는 동사를 수식하며, 〈전치사+명사〉구(전명구)는 주어나 동사를 모두 수식할 수 있다.
수식어는 여러 개 겹쳐 올 수도 있다.

004 The boy (on the left) / suddenly fell down / on the wet floor.
    S   M(전명구: 형용사구)   M(부사)   V   M(전명구: 부사구)
    소년이   (왼쪽에)   갑자기 넘어졌다   젖은 바닥에서.

005 I can't go / to school. My lower back / hurts badly.
    S   V   M(전명구: 부사구) M(형용사) S   V   M(부사)
    나는 갈 수 없다 / 학교에. 내 등 아랫부분이 / 몹시 아프다.

006 Our new teacher from Canada will arrive soon.

007 Some animals like bats and owls sleep during the day.

008 The prize winner's eyes shined with excitement.

3대(기본/빈출/중요) 구문 총망라

● 빈틈없이 탄탄한 구문 실력 완성!
● 1001개의 예문으로 영어 문장 구조와 규칙의 시스템을 완벽히 파악한다!
● 영문을 어구 단위로 끊어 앞에서부터 차례대로 이해하는 해결 능력이
  생겨요!

시작은 우선순위 빈출 구문으로

● 독해에 자주 등장하는 구문만 쏙쏙!
● 단시간 학습으로 최대 효과!
● 500개 알짜배기 예문으로 구문의 기초를 잡으세요!

완성

핵심

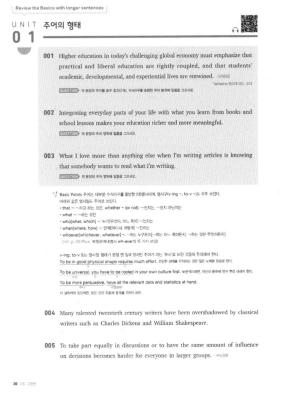

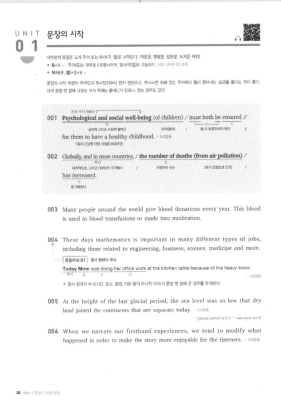

혼동 구문까지 완벽 해결

- 독해에 적용할 때 혼동, 혼란을 줄 수 있는 구문의 집중 해결!
- 비슷한 모양의 구문을 정확히 판별해내는 가장 쉬운 방법 제시!
- 기본편보다 길고 어려운 500개 예문으로 구문의 독해 적용력과 실전 자신감 UP!

실전 고난도 문장 뛰어넘기

- 구문의 단순한 적용으로는 해결이 안 되는 고난도 포인트와 오역 포인트 집중 공략!
- 길고 복잡한 문장은 대부분 독해 문제 해결의 핵심 포인트! 이를 전략적으로 쉽고 빠르게 해결하는 대처법 총망라!
- 500개의 엄선된 예문으로 정확한 구문 분석력과 문장의 핵심을 간파하는, 구문 학습의 궁극적인 목표를 완성해요!

〈천일문 완성〉 학습 로드맵

ROAD MAP

STEP 1 구문 이해하고 적용해보기

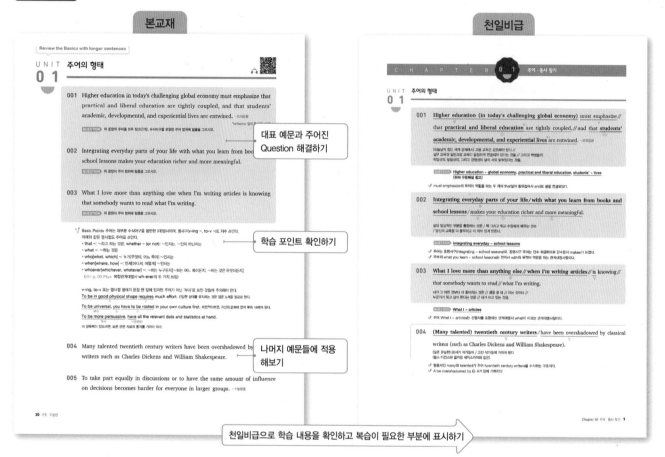

본교재

천일비급

대표 예문과 주어진 Question 해결하기

학습 포인트 확인하기

나머지 예문들에 적용해보기

천일비급으로 학습 내용을 확인하고 복습이 필요한 부분에 표시하기

복습과 반복 학습을 돕는 **연습지** (무료로 다운로드) www.cedubook.com

본문 해석 연습지

영문에 /, // 등의 표시를 하고 해석한 뒤, 천일비급과 대조, 점검한다.

본문 영작 연습지

'빈칸 채우기, 순서 배열하기, 직독직해 뜻을 보며 영작하기'의 세 가지 버전으로 구성되어 있다. 이 중 적절한 것을 골라 우리말을 보고 영문으로 바꿔 써본다.

완성편(Master)의 문장들은 수능 실전에 가깝게 학문적이거나 추상적인 내용의 비중이 크다.
기본편(Basic)이나 핵심편(Essential)에 비해 문장 길이도 수능 실전과 유사하고, 예문 하나에 포함된 구문도 복합적이다.
좀 더 실전 효용성을 더하기 위해 아래와 같이 TOPIC, SUMMARY 등 글의 내용의 핵심을 묻는 문제 등을
주요 독해 문제 유형으로 다양하게 실었다.

> 020 Each time you encounter something new, such as a new piece of music or
> a new language, your brain tries to record as much information as possible,
> paying closer attention to it.
> TOPIC▶ how our brains behave when encountering | unfamiliar / well-known | information

• 문장 요약, 핵심을 파악했는지를 점검할 수 있도록 TOPIC, SUMMARY 등의 문제를 제시하였다. 독해할 때 핵심 주제에 집중하는 능력을 길러줄 것이다.

〈천일문〉은 이들 과정을 돕기 위해 다음과 같은 장치들이 마련되어 있다.

1 암기를 돕는 두 가지 버전의 MP3 파일

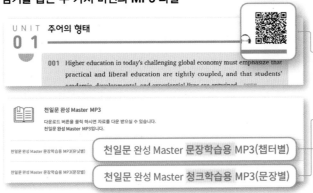

QR 코드 스캔
Unit 제목 옆의 큐알코드를 스캔해 두 가지 버전의 MP3 파일을 재생한다.

www.cedubook.com에서 무료로 다운로드

1 청크 학습: 어구 단위로 끊어 약간 느린 속도로 녹음된 버전. 들으면서 의미를 떠올리고 익숙해질 때까지 반복해서 따라 말한다.

2 문장 학습: 문장 전체를 좀 더 자연스러운 속도로 녹음한 버전. 같은 속도로 따라 말하면서 익힌다.

2 적용을 돕는 〈천일문 완성 문제집 Training Book〉 (별도 판매: 정가 13,000원)

〈완성편〉 본책과는 다른 문장으로 구성되어 있어 구문이 확실하게 학습이 되었는지를 확인/점검해볼 수 있다.
직독직해, 어법, 영작, 해석, 문장전환 등 다양한 유형으로 구성되어 있다. (자세한 정보는 책 뒷면을 참조하세요.)

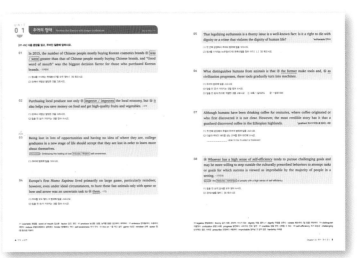

PREVIEW

1 본책

| Must-know Words&Lexical Phrases |

〈핵심 단어와 동 · 반의어, 숙어 등 정리〉

1단계 모르는 것에 표시하고 의미를 익힌다.

2단계 본문 예문을 보면서 의미를 다시 떠올려본다.

기억이 안 날 때는 의미를 확인하여 다시 익힌다.

3단계 부가서비스의 어휘테스트로 확인한다.

(부가서비스의 어휘리스트를 휴대하면서 틈틈이 익힌다.)

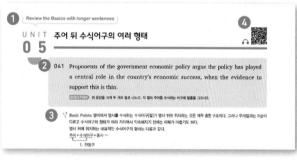

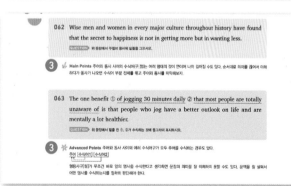

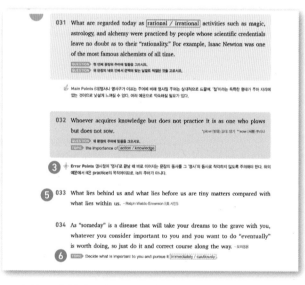

❶ **Review the Basics with longer sentences**
    기본 구문을 좀 더 긴 문장에 적용해보는 워밍업 코너
❷ 대표 예문 예시 & 문제로 알아보는 구문 포인트의 핵심
❸ 학습 포인트 설명
    Ⅴ **Basic Points** 기본 구문 확인
    🖐 **Main Points & ❋ Advanced Points** 주요 구문과 구문 적용이
        다소 어려운 문장에서의 해결 방법
    🖐 **Main Points & ✴ Error Points** 주요 구문과 구문을 잘못 적용
        할 수 있는 경우에 대한 대비 방법

❹ QR코드로 MP3 파일 바로 듣기
❺ 본문 예문으로 적용 훈련: 〈수능〉, 〈모의〉, 〈경찰대〉, 〈사관학교〉 기출
    문장을 포함하여 실전 감각 향상!
❻ 문장의 핵심 이해 확인문제 TOPIC · SUMMARY · FILL-IN 등
    다양한 QUESTION
❼ Plus➕ 구문 이해도를 높여주는 심화 학습 내용

2 천일비급

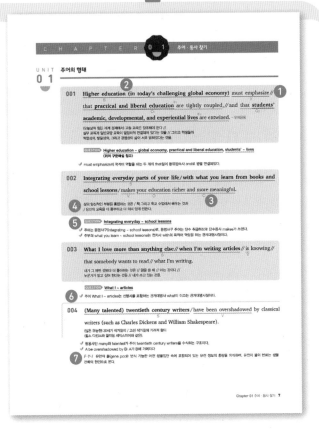

3 무료 부가 서비스

어휘리스트 어휘테스트 해석연습지

딕테이션 Sheet 영작연습지 3종

www.cedubook.com

---

❶ /, // – 끊어 읽기 표시
❷ ( ), [ ] – 수식어구[절] 표시
❸ S, V, O, C, M 구조 분석
❹ 우리말 직역과 필요시 의역

❺ QUESTION 등의 정답 및 해설
❻ 추가 설명
❼ F·Y·I 내용에 대한 추가 정보

일러두기

000 기본 예문 000 고난도 예문
= 동의어, 유의어 ↔ 반의어 ( ) 생략가능 어구·삽입어구 [ ] 대체 가능 어구
to-v to부정사 v-ing 동명사/현재분사 p.p. 과거분사 v 동사원형 또는 원형부정사

〈문장 구조 분석 기호〉

S 주어 V 동사 O 목적어 (IO 간접목적어, DO 직접목적어) C 보어 M 수식어

S′ 종속절의 주어/진주어 V′ 종속절·준동사구 내의 동사 O′ 종속절·준동사구 내의 목적어/진목적어

C′ 종속절·준동사구 내의 보어 M′ 종속절·준동사구 내의 수식어 ( ) 형용사구/생략어구/삽입어구 [ ] 형용사절

S₁(아래첨자) 중복되는 문장 성분 구분

● 본책과 비급의 끊어 읽기 표시(/. //)는 문장구조와 자연스러운 우리말을 고려하여 의미 단위(sense group)를 나타낸 것이다.
원어민들이 실제로 끊어 읽는 곳과는 차이가 있을 수 있다.

● 일반적인 어구의 끊어 읽기는 /로 표시하되, 절과 절의 구별은 //로 표시하였다.
다만, 더 큰 절 내의 부속절은 /로 표시하였다.

　e.g. Kids get super-stressed, // but it isn't always easy to tell / what is bothering them / because they hide symptoms / or explain
them in vague ways.

Move Forward
구조 · 구문편 | 길고 복잡한 문장에 대처하라

Question & Answer

Q1
**구문 학습은
왜 해야 하는 건가요?**

A 구문이란, 수많은 문법 규칙이 모여 이루어진 것 중에서도 특히 자주 나타나는, 영어 특유의 표현 방식을 뜻합니다. 예를 들어 영어는 주어가 길어지는 것을 되도록 피하려고 하지요. 그래서 주어가 길 경우 가주어 it으로 대신하고 진짜 주어는 뒤로 보내므로 〈it ~ that ... 〉등과 같은 영어 특유의 표현 방식, 즉 구문이 나타납니다.

문법에는 수많은 규칙들이 있지만, 독해에는 도움이 되지 않거나 몰라도 크게 상관없는 것들이 많습니다. 위의 예를 든 〈it ~ that ...〉구문의 경우, 문법적으로 보자면 가주어 it과 접속사 that이지만, 이런 분석은 독해할 때 별 의미가 없지요. 이를 구문으로 학습 하면 진짜 주어가 that 이하이므로 이를 주어로 하여 해석하고 이해하는 방법을 익히 게 됩니다. 그러므로 독해를 위해서는 문법이 아니라 구문을 위주로 학습해야 합니다.

Q2
**문장 위주의 학습이
왜 중요한가요?**

A 우리말 설명이 아무리 자세해도 예문이 부족하면 이해가 쉽지 않기 때문입니다. 천 일문은 간단하고 명료한 우리말 설명과 많은 예문으로 구문을 최대한 효과적으로 학습할 수 있도록 구성되었습니다.

Q3
**차라리 독해 문제를 풀면서
구문을 학습하는 것이 좋지
않나요?**

A 평범한 독해 지문은 학습자들이 반드시 학습해야만 하는 구문을 체계적으로 담고 있 지 않아 집중 학습이 불가능하므로 비효율적입니다. 독해 문제를 푸는 것은 어느 정도 구 문 집중 학습을 진행한 뒤에 확인하는 차원에서 진행하는 것이 좋습니다.

Q4
**문장 암기를
꼭 해야 하나요?**

A p.7에서 설명하였듯이 문장 암기는 실전영어를 위한 진정한 능력 향상에 많은 도움 이 됩니다. 외운 문장 그대로를 접하거나 활용할 기회는 많지 않을지 모르지만 기본 구 문을 담은 문장들을 암기하는 것은 어떤 문장도 스스로 해결해나갈 수 있는 능력을 갖추 도록 해줍니다. 또한, 아무리 복잡하고 긴 문장이라 하더라도, 구문 자체가 어렵다기보 다는 여러 기본 구문들이 얽혀 발전되어 나타난 것이기 때문에 기본 구문들은 반드시 자 기 것으로 만드는 것이 중요합니다.

Q5
**시리즈 중 어떤 교재를
선택해야 하나요?**

A 입문-기본-핵심-완성은 점차 난도가 증가하는 동시에 각각의 학습목표가 있습니 다. 중학교 내신 학습이 7, 80%가 된 상태라면 천일문 시리즈를 진행할 수 있습니다.

- **입문** 가장 빈출되는 구문을 쉬운 500개 문장에 담았으므로 빠른 학습이 가능합니다.
- **기본** 기본이 되는 구문을 빠짐없이 1001개 문장에 담아 탄탄한 기본기를 완성할 수 있습니다.
- **핵심** 실전에서 혼동을 주는 구문을 완벽하게 구별하여 정확한 독해를 가능하게 해줍 니다.
- **완성** 복잡하고 긴 문장의 핵심을 요약 정리하는 훈련으로 독해 스피드와 정확성을 올 려줍니다. 수능 고난도 문장과 유사한 수준의 문장을 문제없이 해결 가능합니다.

난도	입문	기본	핵심	완성
어휘	중학 수준	고1 수준	고2 수준	고3 수준 이상
예문 추상성	5%	20%	50%	80%
문장당 구문 개수	1~2개	1~3개	2~5개	3개 이상
문장 길이(평균)	10개 단어	15개 단어	20개 단어	30개 단어

시간에 쫓기는 상황이라면 시리즈 중 본인 수준보다 약간 높은 것을 한 권 택하여 이를 완벽히 소화할 정도로 반복하는 것이 좋습니다.

Q6
내가 끊어 읽은 것과
천일비급의 끊어 읽기가
똑같아야 하나요?

A 천일비급의 끊어 읽기는 의미 단위의 구분을 말하는데, 본인의 끊어 읽기가 천일비급과 다르더라도 해석이 서로 완전히 다르지만 않다면 상관없습니다.

The Sahara Desert kept Egypt isolated / from the rest of the world.
　　　사하라 사막은 이집트를 고립된 상태로 있게 하였다　/　　세계 나머지 나라들로부터. (○)

The Sahara Desert kept Egypt / isolated from the rest of the world.
　　사하라 사막은 이집트를 ~인 채로 있게 하였다　/　세계 나머지 나라들로부터 고립된 상태로. (○)

그러나 아래와 같이 해석이 서로 크게 차이가 나는 것은 문장 전체의 구조 파악에 오류가 있는 것이므로 비급의 의미 단위 구분을 숙지하는 것이 좋겠습니다.

You cannot talk on the phone / in the library / except in designated areas.
　　　당신은 통화를 할 수 없습니다　/　　도서관에서　/　지정된 구역을 제외하고는. (○)

You cannot talk on the phone / in the library except / in designated areas.
　　　당신은 통화를 할 수 없습니다　/　　도서관을 제외하고　/　지정된 구역에서는. (×)

또한, 초보자는 3~4단어 정도로 의미 단위를 구분하고 고급자들은 그보다 훨씬 많은 단어 수로 의미 단위를 구분합니다. 그러므로 본인 수준에 따라 비급보다 더 자주 끊거나 덜 끊는 것은 문제가 되지 않습니다. 본인의 실력이 향상되어감에 따라 의도적으로 의미 단위를 이루는 단어의 수를 점점 늘리는 것이 바람직합니다.

초보자: The best way / to predict the future / is to create it.
중급자: The best way to predict the future / is to create it.

See the Forest

조감편 | 숲을 먼저 보라

기본적인 구문 관련해서는 충분히 학습했다면
구문 학습의 큰 그림에 해당하는 몇 가지 사항들을 종합적인 시각으로
확인한 뒤에 좀 더 심도 있는 학습을 할 필요가 있다.
숲도 보고 나무도 봐야 하지만 앞서 봐야 할 것은 언제나 숲이란 점을 잊지 말자.
이것은 앞으로 세부적인 나무들을 보는 데 믿음직한 안내판 역할을 하게 될 것이다.

기본 문장 구조 **모아 보기**

문장을 이루는 필수 요소인 **주어, 동사, 목적어, 보어**에 각종 **수식어구**가 덧붙는다. 문장 앞뒤에는 부사가 올 수 있는데, 콤마(,)로 구분해주기도 하지만 그렇지 않을 때도 있다.

부사	,	주어	수식어	수식어	동사	수식어
부사		(대)명사	전명구	부사		부사
부사구		명사구	형용사구	부사구		부사구
부사절		명사절	부사(구)	부사절		부사절
			관계사절			

보어	
목적어	
목적어	목적어
목적어	보어
(대)명사	(대)명사
명사구	명사구(절)
명사절	형용사(구)

01 Happiness most often arises from positive relationships with other people.
      ‾‾S‾‾   ‾V‾

02 If you want to make your dreams come true, the first thing you have to do is
                                                ‾‾‾‾‾S‾‾‾‾‾   ‾V‾

   wake up.
   ‾‾C‾‾

03 To apologize sincerely we must first listen attentively to how the other person
   ‾‾‾‾부사구‾‾‾‾ ‾S‾ 조동사 ‾‾V₁‾‾   전치사 ‾‾전치사의 목적어‾‾

   really feels about what happened — not simply assert what we think happened.
                                           ‾‾‾V₂‾‾‾ ‾‾‾‾O₂‾‾‾‾ -수능

04 Traveling gives you many opportunities to consciously connect with the natural
   ‾‾S‾‾ ‾V‾ ‾IO‾   ‾‾‾‾‾‾‾‾‾‾DO‾‾‾‾‾‾‾‾‾‾

   environment, not a zoo or animal park.

05 His reputation as a world-class violinist precedes him and the students consider
                                                              ‾‾‾S‾‾‾ ‾V‾

   him the musician who has influenced them the most. -모의응용
   ‾O‾ ‾‾‾‾‾‾‾‾‾‾‾‾C‾‾‾‾‾‾‾‾‾‾‾‾

06 Politeness makes you enjoyable to be around and so gives you an enduring edge
             ‾V₁‾ ‾O₁‾ ‾‾‾C₁‾‾‾   ‾V₂‾ ‾IO₂‾ ‾‾‾DO₂‾‾‾

   over those who never acquired it. -모의응용

---

01 행복은 다른 사람들과의 긍정적인 관계로부터 가장 자주 생긴다. **02** 꿈을 현실로 이루고 싶다면, 가장 먼저 해야 할 일은 꿈에서 깨어나는 것이다. **03** 진정으로 사과하려면 우리는 우선 상대방이 일어난 일에 대해 정말로 어떻게 느끼는지를 주의 깊게 들어야만 한다. 단순히 우리가 생각하기에 일어난 일을 주장하면 안 된다. **04** 여행하는 것은 여러분에게 동물원이나 야생동물 공원이 아닌 자연환경과 의식적으로 연결할 많은 기회를 준다. **05** 세계적인 바이올린 연주자로서 그의 명성이 앞서고 학생들은 그를 자신들에게 가장 크게 영향을 끼친 음악가로 여긴다. **06** 공손함은 당신을 곁에 있기 즐겁게 만들고, 그래서 그것(공손함)을 절대로 습득하지 못한 사람보다 지속되는 유리함을 당신에게 준다.

❷ 기본 문장 구조의 변형

기본 문장 구조는 여러 가지 이유로 변형이 될 수 있다. 있어야 할 요소가 빠지거나 어순이 변하기도 하며 문장 중간에 어구가 끼어들기도 한다. 단순히 변형되는 형태만 알아둘 것이 아니라 왜 그러한 변형이 일어나는지를 알아두면 글을 좀 더 심도 있게 이해할 수 있다.

1) 생략 (≪ Chapter 05 생략이 일어난 문장 구조 이해하기)

앞에 나온 어구와 똑같이 반복되는 어구는 언어의 경제성을 위해 생략하는 경우가 많다.

01 Health is the greatest gift, **contentment** ✔ **the greatest wealth, faithfulness** ✔ **the best relationship**. –Buddha ((부처)) 〈반복어구 생략〉

02 Taking part in a sports class should be a matter of free choice for the students, **although** ✔ **encouraged by the school**. –모의 〈부사절에서의 주어+be동사 생략〉

2) 어순 변화 (≪ Chapter 06 어순에 주의해야 하는 구문)

영어에서는 강조하고 싶은 어구를 문장 앞으로 보내거나, 길고 중요한 어구를 뒤로 보내기도 한다. 부정어구와 같은 특정 어구가 앞으로 나가면서 주어와 동사의 위치가 바뀌는 도치도 일어난다.

03 <u>How to use our brain efficiently and positively</u> <u>we</u> really <u>should learn</u>.
O S V 〈목적어+주어+동사〉

04 Although **it** is important for a child **to know he is safe**, **it** is also important **to allow a child to experience the instability and uncertainty that comes from competitive situations**. 〈가주어–진주어(to-v)〉

05 <u>Only when your consciousness is totally focused on the moment you are in</u> **can**
only 포함 부사절 조동사
you receive whatever gift, lesson, or delight that moment has to offer.
S V
–Barbara de Angelis ((美 작가)) 〈주어–(조)동사의 도치〉

3) 삽입 (≪ Chapter 10 과감히 건너뛰고 적극적으로 예측하라)

설명을 덧붙이기 위한 부가적 어구를 문장 중간에 끼워 넣기도 한다. ( )로 묶어보면 문장 전체의 구조를 파악하기가 더 쉬워진다.

06 We can learn by asking questions and using instruments, **(such as telescopes or microscopes)**, that let us see or hear far better than with our eyes or ears alone. –모의응용

---

01 건강은 가장 좋은 선물이고, 만족은 가장 좋은 부이며, 충실함은 가장 좋은 관계이다. **02** 체육 수업에 참여하는 것은 비록 학교에서 권장되는 것이더라도, 학생들을 위해서 자유로운 선택의 문제가 되어야 한다. **03** 우리는 두뇌를 능률적이고 긍정적으로 사용하는 방법을 정말로 배워야 한다. **04** 아이가 자신이 안전하다는 것을 아는 것은 중요하지만, 아이가 경쟁적 상황에서 오는 불안정과 불확실을 경험하게 하는 것 또한 중요하다. **05** 당신의 의식이 당신이 있는 그 순간에 온전히 집중되어 있을 때에만 그 순간이 제공하려고 가지고 있는 어떤 선물, 교훈, 또는 기쁨이든 받을 수 있다. **06** 우리는 질문을 하고 우리의 눈이나 귀보다 훨씬 더 잘 보고 들을 수 있게 하는 망원경이나 현미경 같은 도구를 이용하여 배울 수 있다.

준동사의 역할

부정사, 동명사, 분사는 문장에서 명사, 형용사 또는 부사의 역할을 하면서 동사의 성질을 가지므로 준동사라 한다. 준동사는 동사에서 온 것이므로 문장에서 단독으로 오기보다는 목적어나 보어, 수식어 등 딸린 어구와 함께 '구'를 이루는 경우가 많다. 그러므로 문장에서의 역할 외에도 문장 전체에서 준동사구가 어디서부터 어디까지인지를 잘 판단할 수 있어야 한다.

	역할	to-v	v-ing (동명사)	v-ing, p.p. (분사)	분사구문
명사	주어/목적어/보어	✔	✔		
형용사	명사 수식/보어	✔		✔	
부사	동사, 형용사 등 수식	✔			✔

1) 명사 역할 (주어, 목적어, 보어)

01 <u>**To live**</u> is <u>**to suffer**</u>, <u>**to survive**</u> is <u>**to find**</u> some meaning in the suffering.
<small>S₁ C₁ S₂ C₂ −Friedrich Nietzsche ((니체, 독일 철학자))</small>

02 Babies <u>enjoy</u> <u>**cuddling**</u> on a caregiver's lap and <u>**looking**</u> at picture books.
<small>V O₁ O₂</small>

03 In today's world, parenting is <u>about</u> **letting** <u>your child develop into his or her</u>
<small>전치사 전치사의 목적어</small>
<u>own person.</u> −모의

2) 형용사 역할 (명사 수식, 보어)

04 Deserts can be <u>good locations</u> **to farm** solar energy.

05 <u>Changes</u> in seawater chemistry <u>**resulting**</u> from burning of fossil fuels may directly affect deep sea fishes in their larval stages. −모의응용
<small>*larval ((생물)) 어린 유생(幼生)의; 유충의</small>

06 The dream jobs of Korean students <u>have grown</u> more **diversified** thanks to the
<small>V C</small>
influence of the internet and social media outlets.

<small>**01** 산다는 것은 고통 받는 것이고, 생존한다는 것은 그 고통 속에서 어떤 의미를 찾는 것이다. **02** 아기들은 돌봐주는 사람의 무릎 위에 꼭 붙어 있는 것과 그림책을 보는 것을 즐거워한다. **03** 오늘날의 세상에서, 육아는 아이가 자신의 인격체로 발전하도록 하는 것에 관한 것이다. **04** 사막은 태양 에너지를 만들어내기 좋은 장소가 될 수 있다. **05** 화석 연료 연소로 발생한 바닷물의 화학 성분의 변화는 심해 어류가 유생 단계에 있을 때 직접적으로 영향을 미칠 수 있다. **06** 한국 학생들의 꿈의 직업은 인터넷과 소셜 미디어 표현 수단의 영향 덕분에 더욱 다양해졌다.</small>

07 Genetic tracking through generations helps doctors **to predict** the likelihood of
<u>O</u>
a person getting a disease and **to diagnose** it — although not to cure the
<u>C</u>
illness. – 모의응용

08 Sunglasses keep <u>our eyes</u> **protected** from strong sunlight, particularly UV
<u>O</u>   <u>C</u>
rays, so they are a must-have accessory for maintaining healthy vision.

3) 부사 역할

09 Don't lower your expectations **to meet** <u>your performance</u>. Raise your level of
M
performance **to meet** <u>your expectations</u>.
M

10 All forms of life are closely related to each other, **<u>nourishing and protecting</u>**
M
<u>each other</u>.

11 **<u>Faced with a problem you do not understand</u>**, do any part of it you do
M
understand, and then go back to it later.

4

명사절, 형용사절, 부사절

문장에서 명사, 형용사, 부사 역할을 하지만 주어-동사를 갖춘 어구를 '절'이라고 한다. 절의 역할에 따라 사용할 연결사는 무엇이고 어떤 의미인지를 잘 이해하여 적용해야 한다. 특히 명사절과 형용사절의 경우, 문장 전체에서 절이 어디서부터 어디까지인지를 잘 판단할 수 있어야 한다.

종류	역할	연결사
명사절	주어/목적어/보어	접속사 that, whether, if, 의문사, 관계대명사 what, whatever 등
형용사절	명사(선행사) 수식	앞에 콤마(,) 없는 관계사절
부사절	동사, 형용사, 주절 등 수식	접속사 when, because, if, although, so that, as 등

1) 명사절

문장에서 꼭 필요한 요소인 주어, 목적어, 보어 역할을 한다. 그러므로 문장에서 명사절을 삭제하면 문장이 성립하지 않는다는 것도 함께 알아두도록 하자.

01 **What** is true today may not be true tomorrow, and **what** is accepted in our
   _{S₁}   _{S₂}
society may not be accepted in other societies.

02 The early stages of a pandemic can be especially anxiety-provoking because
you don't know **how** widespread or deadly the illness is going to be during this
      V   O
time.

03 The important idea we should fix firmly in mind is **that** our self-image is
                                                          C
formed by our beliefs, not simply by our past experiences. —수능응용

---

01 오늘 사실인 것이 내일은 사실이 아닐지도 모른다. 그리고 우리 사회에서 받아들여지는 것이 다른 사회에서는 받아들여지지 않을 지도 모른다. **02** 전국적 유행병의 초기 단계는 특히 불안을 일으킬 수 있는데, 그 병이 그동안 얼마나 널리 퍼질지 또는 얼마나 치명적일지 모르기 때문이다. **03** 우리가 마음에 확고히 새겨야 할 중요한 생각은 우리의 자아상이 단지 과거의 경험에 의해서가 아니라, 우리의 믿음에 의해 형성된다는 것이다.

2) 형용사절

선행사를 수식한다. 막연한 의미의 선행사를 구체적으로 밝혀주는 것이므로 선행사를 이해하는 데 꼭 필요한 정보이다.

04 During the early 1980s, a team of Italian scientists found that people seem to have one foot **that** is more ticklish than the other — and for most people it is the right. -모의응용

05 Technological development often forces change, and change is uncomfortable. This is one of the main reasons **why** technology is often resisted and **why** some perceive it as a threat. -모의

3) 부사절

문장에서 부사의 역할을 하면서, '시간·원인·조건·양보·목적·결과·양태' 등의 의미를 나타낸다. 부사절이 주절 뒤에 올 때는 앞에 콤마(,)가 없는 경우가 많다는 것과, 부사절에서 접속사를 제외한 나머지는 주어-동사 등이 갖추어진 완전한 구조의 절이라는 것도 함께 알아두자.

06 The best moments usually occur **when** a person's body or mind is stretched to its limits in a voluntary effort to accomplish something difficult and worthwhile. -수능 〈시간〉

07 Remember not to write every word, **as** this might interfere with your complete understanding of the speaker. -사관학교 〈원인〉

08 **If** deforestation persists at the pace it's occurring, we won't have a lot of the beneficial remaining forestry. 〈조건〉   *forestry 삼림지

09 **Although** the world is full of suffering, it is full also of the overcoming of it.
                                                            -Helen Keller 〈양보〉

10 **Just as** one gesture can have many different meanings, so many different gestures can have the same meaning. 〈양태〉

---

04 1980년대 초반, 이탈리아 과학자들로부터 구성된 한 (연구)팀은 사람들이 다른 발보다 더 간지럼을 타는 발이 있는 것 같음을 발견했고, 대부분 사람들에게 있어 그것은 오른발이라는 것도 발견했다. **05** 과학 기술의 발전은 흔히 변화를 강요하는데, 변화는 불편하다. 이것이 과학 기술이 흔히 저항을 받고 일부 사람들이 그것을 위협으로 인식하는 주된 이유 중 하나이다. **06** 최고의 순간들은 어렵고 가치 있는 어떤 것을 성취하려는 자발적인 노력 속에서 한 사람의 신체나 정신이 그 한 계점까지 이를 때 보통 일어난다. **07** 모든 단어를 받아 적지 않을 것을 기억하라. 이것이 화자의 말을 완전히 이해하는 것을 방해할지도 모르기 때문이다. **08** 삼림 벌채가 일어나고 있는 속도를 지속된다면, 우리는 이익을 주는 남아 있는 삼림지를 많이 가질 수 없을 것이다. **09** 비록 세상은 고통으로 가득 차 있지만, 고통을 극복하는 일로도 가득 차 있다. **10** 한 가지 몸짓이 많은 다양한 의미를 가질 수 있는 것과 마찬가지로, 많은 다양한 몸짓들이 같은 의미를 가질 수 있다.

상관어구

어떤 어구가 오면 그와 짝을 이루는 다른 어구가 뒤에 이어질 것이 예상되는 구문이 있다. 이들을 잘 알아두면 독해할 때 문장 구조나 의미를 좀 더 쉽게 알 수 있어 매우 유용하다. 가주어 및 가목적어 구문과 상관구문, 그리고 전명구를 동반하는 동사 구문이 이에 해당한다.

1) 가주어/가목적어 (≪ Unit 41)

01 To stop severe bleeding **it** is essential **to put pressure on the wound right away**, and do not remove the pressure until medical professionals arrive.

02 We need to make **it** a rule of life **never to regret anything**; it's just a waste of time.

2) 상관접속사 (≪ Unit 42)

03 Success is **neither** magical **nor** mysterious. Success is the natural consequence of consistently applying the basic fundamentals. –Jim Rohn ((美 기업가))

04 The original idea of a patent, remember, was **not** to reward inventors with monopoly profits, **but** to encourage them to share their inventions. –모의

05 The effects of color blindness are **so** mild **that** many boys only realize that they have it at a relatively late age.

3) 상관대명사 (≪ Unit 43)

일부 대명사들은 앞에 나온 명사에 대해 짝을 이루어 지칭하기도 한다.

06 Do not trust all men, but trust men of worth; **the former** course is silly, **the latter** a mark of prudence. –Democritus ((고대 그리스 철학자))

07 There are only two ways to live your life. **One** is as though nothing is a miracle. **The other** is as though everything is a miracle. –Albert Einstein

4) 전명구를 동반하는 동사 (≪ Unit 44)

08 The minimum wage laws may be the only way to **prevent** many employees **from** working at wages that are below the poverty line. –모의

---

01 심각한 출혈을 멈추기 위해 상처 위에 즉시 압박을 가하는 것이 매우 중요하며, 전문 의료진이 도착할 때까지 압박을 멈추지 마라. **02** 우리는 절대 아무것도 후회하지 않는 것을 삶의 원칙으로 해야 한다. 그것(후회)은 그저 시간 낭비이다. **03** 성공은 마술적인 것도 불가사의한 것도 아니다. 성공은 기본 원칙들을 끊임없이 적용하는 것의 자연스러운 결과이다. **04** 특허권의 원래 목적은, 발명가에게 독점 이익을 보상하는 것이 아니라 그들이 발명품을 공유하도록 장려하는 것임을 기억하라. **05** 색맹의 영향은 매우 약해서 많은 소년들이 자신들이 색맹이라는 것을 상대적으로 늦은 나이가 되어서야 깨닫는다. **06** 모든 사람을 믿지 말고, 가치 있는 사람을 믿어라. 전자의 방침은 어리석으며, 후자는 분별력의 표시이다. **07** 삶을 사는 오직 두 가지 방식이 있다. 하나는 마치 어떤 것도 기적이 아닌 것처럼 사는 것이다. 다른 하나는 마치 모든 것이 기적인 것처럼 사는 것이다. **08** 최저임금법은 많은 노동자들이 빈곤선 아래의 월급으로 노동하는 것을 방지하는 유일한 방법일지도 모른다.

6

요소의 나열

문장을 이루는 주어, 동사, 목적어, 수식어는 등위접속사나 콤마(,)로 나열되어 문장이 길어지는 원인이 되기도 한다. 중요한 것은 <u>등위접속사가 무엇과 무엇을 연결하는지</u>를 파악하는 것이다. 특히, 절과 절을 연결하는 경우도 적지 않으므로 등위접속사 주변만 보지 말고 문장을 전체적으로 보는 시각이 필요하다.

01 Human beings have long depended on the cooperation of others for the <u>supply of food</u>, <u>protection from predators</u>, [and] <u>the acquisition of essential knowledge.</u> −모의

02 My father's belief was <u>that life has its ups and downs</u> [and] <u>that each person has to come to terms with his or her own share of misery.</u>

03 We keep <u>moving forward</u>, <u>opening new doors</u>, [and] <u>doing new things</u>, because <u>we're curious</u> [and] <u>curiosity keeps leading us down new paths.</u> −Walt Disney

04 <u>The mind has great influence over the body,</u> [and] <u>diseases often have their origin there.</u> −Moliere ((프랑스 극작가))

05 <u>I disapprove of what you say,</u> [but] <u>I will defend to the death your right to say it.</u>
−Evelyn Beatrice Hall ((英 작가))

06 <u>"Defensive pessimism," a strategy of imagining the worst-case scenario of any situation, can be useful,</u> [for] <u>indulging in negative thoughts actually helps people go on to do their best by preparing for the worst.</u> −모의응용

---

01 인간은 식량의 공급, 포식자로부터의 보호, 그리고 필수적인 지식의 습득을 위해 타인들의 협력에 오랫동안 의존해 왔다. **02** 나의 아버지의 믿음은 인생에는 기복이 있다는 것, 그리고 사람은 자기 몫의 불행을 감수해야 한다는 것이었다. **03** 우리는 계속해서 앞으로 나아가고, 새로운 문들을 열고, 새로운 일들을 하는데, 왜냐하면 우리는 호기심이 많고, 호기심은 우리를 계속해서 새로운 길로 안내하기 때문이다. **04** 정신은 신체에 대단한 영향을 미치고, 질병은 종종 거기서 비롯된다. **05** 나는 당신이 말하는 것에 찬성하지 않지만, 그것을 말할 당신의 권리를 나는 목숨을 걸고 지킬 것이다. **06** 어느 상황이든 최악의 시나리오를 상상해보는 전략인 '방어적 비관주의'는 유용할 수 있는데, 왜냐하면 부정적인 생각에 빠지는 것이 최악의 상황을 대비함으로써 실제로 사람들이 최선을 다해 나아가도록 돕기 때문이다.

부연 설명

앞에 나온 어구에 대한 부연 설명을 이끄는 구문으로는 콤마(,) 다음에 나오는 관계사, 삽입구문, 세미콜론(;) 다음에 나오는 that is와 in other words 등이 있다. 이들 부연 설명은 대부분 부가적 정보에 해당하므로, 앞에 나온 어구를 충분히 이해했다면 이 부분을 읽지 않고 건너뛰어도 무방하다. 단, 동격구문이나 콜론(:) 뒤의 내용이 앞에 나온 막연한 의미의 어구를 구체적으로 밝혀서 설명할 때는 읽고 이해하는 것이 좋다.

01 Costa Rica was discovered in 1502 and named by *Christopher Columbus*, **who thought it might be a land rich in gold.** – 모의응용

02 Some earthquakes are produced *before or during volcanic activity*, **when rock is moving to fill in spaces where magma is no longer present.**

03 *Alfred Nobel*, **the inventor of dynamite**, died childless in 1896 and dedicated his vast fortune to creating the Nobel Prizes.

04 To justify the time and effort needed to fully understand a work of literature in a foreign language, there must be *some special incentives involved* — **enjoyment, suspense, or fresh insights into important matters.** – 경찰대응용

05 *The Harry Potter books*, **written by author J. K. Rowling**, are loved by millions of readers from the very young to the very old.

06 Coevolution is the concept that two or more species of organisms can reciprocally influence the evolutionary direction of the other. **In other words,** organisms affect the evolution of other organisms. – 모의

07 Most teachers are of *the opinion* **that children learn through interaction, by listening to others and discussing ideas with them.**

08 Concentration is a mental skill you can develop. There are *two ways to improve your concentration*: First, raise your brain's natural ability to concentrate. Second, adjust the environment around you to make concentrating easier.

---

01 코스타리카는 1502년에 발견되었고 크리스토퍼 콜럼버스에 의해 이름 지어졌는데, 그는 그곳이 금이 풍부한 땅일 수도 있다고 생각했다. **02** 일부 지진은 화산 활동 전이나 도중에 발생하는데, 그때 암석이 마그마가 더는 (채우고) 있지 않은 공간을 채우기 위해 움직이고 있기 때문이다. **03** 다이너마이트의 발명가인 알프레드 노벨은 1896년에 자녀 없이 사망했고 노벨상을 제정하는 데 그의 막대한 재산을 바쳤다. **04** 외국어로 된 문학 작품을 완전히 이해하는 데 필요한 시간과 노력을 정당화하기 위해서, 그와 관련된 특별한 유인책이 있어야 한다. 즉, 즐거움, 긴장감, 또는 중요한 문제에 대한 새로운 통찰이 그것들이다. **05** 해리 포터 소설은 작가 J. K. 롤링에 의해 쓰였는데, 아주 어린 아이들부터 매우 나이 많은 사람들에 이르기까지 수백만 독자들에게 사랑 받는다. **06** 공진화는 둘 혹은 그 이상의 생물종이 다른 종의 진화 방향에 상호적으로 영향을 미칠 수 있다는 개념이다. 다시 말해서, 유기체는 다른 유기체의 진화에 영향을 미친다. **07** 대부분의 교사는 아이들이 다른 사람들의 이야기를 듣고 그들과 생각을 나누면서 상호작용을 통해서 배운다고 생각한다. **08** 집중은 발전시킬 수 있는 정신적 능력이다. 정신 집중을 개선하는 데는 두 가지 방법이 있다. 첫 번째로, 두뇌의 타고난 집중 능력을 높여라. 두 번째로, 집중하는 것을 더 쉽게 하기 위해 여러분 주변 환경을 조정하라.

끊어읽기

문장을 직독직해하기 위해서는 문장을 구성하는 요소들을 의미 단위별로 끊어 읽는 것이 필요하다. 주요한 끊어 읽기 요령은 다음과 같다.

A. 주어가 긴 경우에는 주어 다음에서 끊는다. 대개 동사 앞까지가 주어에 해당한다. 주어에 절이 포함된 경우, 주어 부분에 있는 동사를 문장 전체의 동사로 혼동하지 않도록 주의한다.
B. 구나 절의 형식을 한 긴 목적어나 보어의 앞에서 끊는다.
C. 긴 수식어의 앞 또는 뒤에서 끊는다.
D. 접속사 앞에서 끊는다.

01 The man who doesn't read good books / has no advantage / over the man who
　　　좋은 책을 읽지 않는 사람은　　　　　　　　　/　　유리한 점이 없다　　/

can't read them. – Mark Twain ((美 작가))
책을 읽을 수 없는 사람보다.

02 It is widely believed // that the impact of a giant meteorite / caused
　　(~은) 널리 받아들여진다　　　//　　　　거대한 운석의 충돌이　　　　　/

a mass extinction of life that included the dinosaurs, / 65 million years ago.
　　공룡을 포함한 생명체의 대량 멸종을 일으켰다는 것.　　　/　　6천5백만 년 전에.　　– 경찰대응용

03 Think about readers' wants, needs, values, and concerns, // and decide
　　　　독자의 욕구, 필요, 가치, 그리고 걱정에 대해 생각하라.　　　　　//

what your writing can do / to meet their needs or resolve their concerns.
그리고 당신의 글이 무엇을 할 수 있을지 결정하라 /　　그들의 필요를 충족하거나 그들의 걱정을 해결하기 위해.

04 Doctors are starting to find / more and more information / that suggests
　　의사들은 발견하기 시작하고 있다　　/　　더욱더 많은 정보를　　/

a connection between exercise and brain development. – 모의
　　　운동과 두뇌 발달 사이의 연관성을 시사하는.

05 Study the lives of the great people / who have made an impact on the world, //
　　위대한 사람들의 삶을 연구하라　　/　　　　세상에 영향을 끼친.　　　//

and you will find / that in virtually every case, / they spent a considerable
그러면 여러분은 알게 될 것이다 /　　사실상 모든 경우에 있어서,　　/

amount of time alone thinking. – 모의
그들이 상당한 양의 시간을 혼자 생각하는 데에 보냈다는 것.

See the Trees

구조·구문편 | 나무를 보라

숲은 전체 흐름을 보여줄 수 있지만 문제의 해결은 각각의 나무를 들여다봐야 나올 때가 많다.
문장 하나하나를 자세히 들여다보고, 왜 이 문장은 구조 파악이 어려운 것인지
왜 이 구문을 인지하지 못한 것인지를 분석하고 알아보아야 해결책이 나온다.

주어 · 동사 찾기

Chapter Overview

● 문장의 기본 골격을 이루는 것은 '주어-동사'이다. 따라서 문장에서 주어-동사를 찾는 것이 독해의 시작이자 핵심이다.

● 주어의 다양한 형태와 문장이 수식어구로 시작하여 주어를 찾기 어려운 경우, 주어 부분이 매우 길어서 동사를 찾기 어려운 경우에 대해 알아본다.

Chapter Goals

1 (대)명사 외에 주어가 될 수 있는 명사구의 형태 두 가지를 말할 수 있다.

2 명사절을 이끄는 연결사를 열거할 수 있다.

3 수식어구[절] 내의 명사를 주어로 착각하지 않고 주어를 바르게 파악할 수 있다.

4 명사구나 명사절의 범위를 정확히 판단하여 동사를 파악할 수 있다.

Must-know
Words &
Lexical
Phrases

UNIT01 •

001 liberal (일반)교양의; 자유민주적인; 진보적인

    cf. **liberal arts** 교양과목

    couple 연결하다; 두 사람; 커플

    developmental 발달상의

    experiential 경험에 의한, 경험상의

002 integrate A with B A를 B와 통합하다

004 overshadow (~의 그늘에 가려) 빛을 잃게[무색하게] 만들다;

    가리다, 그늘지게 하다

006 ensure 보장하다

    look into ~을 검토하다, ~을 조사하다

    enforce (법률 등을) 시행하다

    regulation 규정, 단속

    violate 위반하다; 침해하다

007 evolutionary 진화의

    countless 셀 수 없이 많은, 무수한

    organism 생물체, 유기체

    conserve 보존하다

    collective 집단적인

008 sibling 형제자매

009 national border 국경

    volume 양, 생산량; 대량; 부피; (책 등의) 권

    fuel 활기를 불어넣다; 연료를 공급하다

010 foolery 어리석음; 어리석은 짓

    trivial 하찮은, 사소한

UNIT02 •

011 interactive 쌍방향의, 상호작용을 하는

    real-time 실시간의

    dominance 지배; 우월

012 on a daily basis 매일

    settlement 거주지, 정착지; 해결, 조정

014 nonverbal 비언어적인, 말로 하지 않는 (↔verbal 언어의, 말로 하는)

015 impressive 인상적인

    subtle 감지하기 어려운, 미묘한; 예리한

detection 탐지, 발견

cf. detect 탐지하다, 발견하다

scope 범위; 시야; 샅샅이 조사하다

016 numerous 수많은

018 extensive 대규모[광범위]의, 넓은 범위에 걸친

019 disturb 불안하게 만들다; 방해하다

mingle with ~와 섞다

UNIT 03 •

021 validate 확인하다; 옳음을 증명하다; (법적으로) 유효하게 하다

022 scattered 흩어진, 드문드문 있는

randomly 일정하지 않게, 임의로

be made up of ~로 이루어져 있다, ~로 구성되다

023 brilliant 놀라운, 멋진; 눈부신; 재능이 뛰어난

astound 깜짝 놀라게 하다 (=shock, astonish)

024 faith 믿음, 신념

exceptional 예외적인; 이례적인, 비범한

phenomenon ((복수형 phenomena)) 현상; 경이로운 것

rational 합리적인; 이성적인 (↔irrational 비이성[비논리]적인)

cf. rationality 합리성; 이치에 맞음

insight 통찰력; 지각 (=perception)

025 think straight 논리적으로[명쾌하게] 사고하다

026 soothing 마음에 안정을 주는, 진정시키는

restful 편안한, 평화로운

027 by-product 부산물 ((부수적으로 생기는 물건이나 현상)); 부작용

potent 강력한, 중요한 (=powerful)

inspire 격려하다, 분발하게 하다; 영감을 주다

permit A to-v A가 v하게 허용하다

028 satirical 풍자적인

cf. satire 풍자, 비꼼

029 acquire A from B A를 B에게서 얻다

acquaintance 지인, 아는 사람

fill (어떤 역할을) 수행하다; 충족시키다; 채우다

UNIT 04 •

031 regard A as B A를 B로 여기다

astrology 점성술

alchemy 연금술; (물건을 변질시키는) 마력

cf. alchemist 연금술사

credential ((주로 복수형)) 자격(증); 신뢰할 수 있는; 자격증을 주다

as to A A에 관해서

of all time 역사상, 지금껏

034 along[on] the way 중간에, 도중에

pursue 추구하다

035 extraterrestrial 외계의, 지구 밖의; 외계인, 우주인

burning question[issue] 의견이 분분한 문제

036 controversy 논쟁, 논란

cf. controversial 논란이 많은

be associated with ~와 관련이 있다

slavery 노예 (제도)

037 reach an agreement with ~와 합의에 도달하다

039 evaluate 평가하다, 감정하다

040 launch 발사(하다); 시작(하다); 출시(하다)

remote 외진 (=isolated); 멀리 떨어진 (=distant)

location 지역; 위치

cf. located in ~에 위치된

counterintuitive 직관에 반대되는

(↔intuitive 직관적인, 직감에 의한; 이해하기 쉬운)

cf. counter- 반대를 의미하는 접두사

futuristic 선진적인, 미래의; 초현대적인

UNIT 01 주어의 형태

001 Higher education in today's challenging global economy must emphasize that practical and liberal education are tightly coupled, and that students' academic, developmental, and experiential lives are entwined. —모의응용

*entwine 얽히게 하다, 꼬다

QUESTION ▶ 위 문장의 주어를 모두 찾고(3개), 수식어구를 포함한 주어 범위에 밑줄을 그으시오.

002 Integrating everyday parts of your life with what you learn from books and school lessons makes your education richer and more meaningful.

QUESTION ▶ 위 문장의 주어 범위에 밑줄을 그으시오.

003 What I love more than anything else when I'm writing articles is knowing that somebody wants to read what I'm writing.

QUESTION ▶ 위 문장의 주어 범위에 밑줄을 그으시오.

▽ **Basic Points** 주어는 대부분 수식어구를 동반한 (대)명사이며, 명사구(v-ing ~, to-v ~)도 자주 쓰인다.
아래와 같은 명사절도 주어로 쓰인다.
- that ~: ~라고 하는 것은, whether ~ (or not): ~인지는, ~인지 아닌지는
- what ~: ~하는 것은
- who(m)[what, which] ~: 누가[누구를, 무엇이, 어느 쪽이] ~하는지는
- when[where, how, why] ~: 언제[어디서, 어떻게, 왜] ~하는지는
- whoever[whichever, whatever] ~: ~하는 누구든지[~하는 어느 쪽이든지, ~하는 것은 무엇이든지]
(◁ p. 31 Plus 복합관계대명사 wh-ever의 두 가지 쓰임)

v-ing, to-v 또는 명사절 형태가 문장 맨 앞에 있지만 주어가 아닌 '부사'로 쓰인 것들에 주의해야 한다.
To be in good physical shape requires much effort. 건강한 상태를 유지하는 것은 많은 노력을 필요로 한다.
      S   V
To be universal, you have to be rooted in your own culture first. 보편적이려면, 자신의 문화에 먼저 뿌리 내려야 한다.
  부사   S   V
To be more persuasive, have all the relevant data and statistics at hand.
    부사   V(명령문)
더 설득력이 있으려면, 모든 관련 자료와 통계를 가까이 하라.

004 Many talented twentieth century writers have been overshadowed by classical writers such as Charles Dickens and William Shakespeare.

005 To take part equally in discussions or to have the same amount of influence on decisions becomes harder for everyone in larger groups. —수능응용

006 To ensure the safety of students who use electric scooters on campus, as well as those around them, officials should look into enforcing stricter regulations, such as giving students a warning when they violate the regulations. −모의응용

QUESTION▶ 위 문장의 주어에 밑줄을 그으시오.

007 As evolutionary scholar Henry Plotkin says, gaining knowledge of the world across countless generations, organisms conserve knowledge selectively based on evolutionary need, and that collective knowledge is then held within the gene pool of species. −경찰대응용

008 Whether I am a good son/daughter or not depends partly on the way in which I behave to my parents, but partly, and no less importantly, on the relationships I have with my siblings.

009 Whether companies buy or sell products across national borders, these businesses are all contributing to the volume of international trade that is fueling the global economy. −사관학교응용

010 Whoever wants music instead of noise, joy instead of pleasure, soul instead of gold, creative work instead of business, passion instead of foolery, finds no home in this trivial world of ours. −Hermann Hesse ((헤르만 헤세, 소설가))

SUMMARY▶ In our world, it is tough / reasonable to live a meaningful life.

Plus⁺ 복합관계대명사 wh-ever의 두 가지 쓰임

복합관계대명사는 명사절이나 부사절을 이끈다. 명사절은 문장에서 주어, 목적어, 보어 역할을 하므로 삭제하면 문장이 성립하지 않지만, 부사절은 삭제해도 문장이 성립한다. 복합관계대명사가 이끄는 명사절과 부사절은 의미도 서로 다르다.

	명사절	부사절
whoever	~하는 누구든지 (= anyone who)	누가 ~하더라도 (= no matter who)
whichever	~하는 어느 것이든지 (= any(thing) that)	어느 것을 ~하더라도 (= no matter which)
whatever	~하는 무엇이든지 (= any(thing) that)	무엇을 ~하더라도 (= no matter what)

Whatever is begun in anger ends in shame. −Benjamin Franklin ((美 과학자, 정치가))
 S   V

분노로 시작된 **것은 무엇이든지** 수치심으로 끝난다.

Whatever I do, I will do on my own.
  부사절   S   V

내가 **무엇을 하더라도**, 나는 내 힘으로 할 것이다.

011 In an interactive, real-time strategy video game set in the 26th century, hundreds of thousands of players spend up to 80 hours a week fighting inter-species battles for dominance and survival.

QUESTION 위 문장의 주어(형용사 수식어구 포함)에 밑줄을 그으시오.

🖋️ **Main Points** 부사구로 시작하는 문장은 대부분 〈부사구+콤마(,)+주어+동사 ~〉의 형태이다. 부사구와 주어 사이에 대개 콤마(,)를 두므로 쉽게 구별할 수 있다. (위의 예문과 같이 부사구 내에서도 콤마가 있을 수 있으므로 무조건 콤마 뒤를 주어로 판단하지 않도록 주의한다.)

012 In a village where the houses are all grouped closely together fifty-three per cent of the visiting between families was on a daily basis, whereas in a settlement where the houses are spread out only thirty-four per cent of the visiting was on a daily basis. –사관학교응용

QUESTION 위 문장을 두 개의 절로 나누고, 각 절의 주어(형용사 수식어구 포함)에 밑줄을 그으시오.
SUMMARY ⃞Distance / Relationship⃞ is an important factor in determining rate of interaction.

013 Every year millions of young people finish school feeling full of confidence and arrive in the workplace only to find out how much they don't know.

QUESTION 위 문장의 주어(형용사 수식어구 포함)에 밑줄을 그으시오.

✳️ **Advanced Points** 부사구와 주어 사이에는 콤마가 없을 수도 있다. 또한, 명사 형태지만 시간이나 장소를 뜻하는 부사로 쓰이는 어구가 문장 맨 앞에 나올 수도 있으므로 주의한다.

014 Due to lack of understanding of cultural differences in expression, interpretation of nonverbal behavior may be ⃞accurate / inaccurate⃞ in addition to verbal communication.

QUESTION 위 문장의 네모 안에서 문맥에 맞는 낱말로 적절한 것을 고르시오.

015 In spite of the impressive gains of environmental regulation, new and more subtle sources of pollution and better methods of detection have made us aware of the broad scope of our pollution problems.

016 With access to a whole range of discounts on numerous facilities, including a sports center, a health center, theaters and museums, students can save a good amount of money.

017 During the 18th century the majority of industries in Europe still relied on wind and water power as well as horse and man-power to drive their small machines.

018 In the developed world the widespread use of water-based toilets from the mid-nineteenth century meant that extensive, connected systems of sewage pipes sending the outflow into sewage processing plants were built in cities.

－사관학교

*sewage 하수, 오물 **outflow (액체 등의) 유출(물)

019 One morning, I was suddenly disturbed by a fire alarm, mingled with the shouts and footsteps of people.

020 Each time you encounter something new, such as a new piece of music or a new language, your brain tries to record as much information as possible, paying closer attention to it.

TOPIC how our brains behave when encountering ⌈unfamiliar / well-known⌉ information

021 Seeing only the good in one's own actions and the bad in those of others is a common human weakness, and validating only the positive or negative aspects of the human experience is not productive. – 사관학교

QUESTION 위 문장을 두 개의 절로 나누고 각 절의 주어 범위에 밑줄을 그으시오.

🖋 **Main Points** 명사구가 문장의 주어일 때, 주어를 이루는 범위는 일반적으로 동사가 나오기 전까지이다. v-ing와 to-v는 원래 동사에서 나온 것이므로 뒤에 목적어, 보어, 부사(구)가 길게 이어질 수 있다.

022 To imagine that the Arab World is a giant desert with cities and villages scattered randomly throughout would be like saying that the United States is made up of country towns run by cowboys. – 모의응용

QUESTION 위 문장의 주어 범위에 밑줄을 그으시오.
SUMMARY People have a(n) complete / incomplete picture of the Arab World.

023 Making a coin disappear from a glass is a simple but brilliant magic trick that always leaves the audience astounded with surprise and delight.

QUESTION 위 문장의 주어 범위에 밑줄을 그으시오.

✳ **Error Points** 명사구 내에 포함된 p.p.(특히 동사의 과거형과 같은 형태인 것)나 원형부정사 등을 문장 전체의 동사로 착각하지 말아야 한다. 과거분사(p.p.)는 앞의 명사를 수식하거나 목적격보어로 쓰일 수 있고, 원형부정사 역시 목적격보어로 쓰일 수 있다.

024 To have faith in the possibility of love as not only an exceptional-individual phenomenon but also a social phenomenon, is a rational faith based on the insight into the very nature of man. – Erich Fromm ((美 사회심리학자))

025 Reading speed is important, but being able to think straight about what you read is far more valuable.

026 After a stressful day, relaxing in a comfortable chair, putting on some soothing sounds, and reading something light and entertaining are all good methods to get ready for some restful sleep. – 모의응용

027 Creating an environment where learning and its natural by-product, mistakes, are okay can be a potent tool to unite a group and inspire creativity, risk-taking, and effort. –사관학교응용

SUMMARY ▶ A group that permits / warns its members to make mistakes gets more positive results.

028 Because humans consider themselves the highest form of life and therefore better than any other animal, showing animals speaking and behaving like humans in movies and books is a useful _____ tool to show human behavior to be more animal-like than we like to admit.

FILL-IN ▶ ① complimentary   ② satirical

029 A background check of new employees acquires / acquired from acquaintances or coworkers of their previous company depending on their responsibilities in the job they are filling is a common practice.

QUESTION ▶ 위 문장의 네모 안에서 적절한 것을 고르시오.

030 Watching friends struggle before they ask for help may be hard, but it's much better to be patient and make sure that your door is always open.

031 What are regarded today as rational / irrational activities such as magic, astrology, and alchemy were practiced by people whose scientific credentials leave no doubt as to their "rationality." For example, Isaac Newton was one of the most famous alchemists of all time.

QUESTION 첫 번째 문장의 주어에 밑줄을 그으시오.
QUESTION 위 문장의 네모 안에서 문맥에 맞는 낱말로 적절한 것을 고르시오.

Main Points (대)명사나 명사구가 이끄는 주어에 비해 명사절 주어는 상대적으로 드물며, '절'이라는 독특한 형태가 주어 자리에 있는 것이므로 낯설게 느껴질 수 있다. 여러 예문으로 익숙해질 필요가 있다.

032 Whoever acquires knowledge but does not practice it is as one who plows but does not sow.

*plow (밭을) 갈다; 쟁기 **sow (씨를) 뿌리다

QUESTION 위 문장의 주어에 밑줄을 그으시오.
TOPIC the importance of action / knowledge

Error Points 명사절이 '명사'로 끝날 때 바로 이어지는 문장의 동사를 그 '명사'의 동사로 착각하지 않도록 주의해야 한다. 위의 예문에서 it은 practice의 목적어이므로, is의 주어가 아니다.

033 What lies behind us and what lies before us are tiny matters compared with what lies within us. —Ralph Waldo Emerson ((美 시인))

034 As "someday" is a disease that will take your dreams to the grave with you, whatever you consider important to you and you want to do "eventually" is worth doing, so just do it and correct course along the way. —모의응용

TOPIC Decide what is important to you and pursue it immediately / cautiously.

035 Whether extraterrestrial life has actually touched the soil of Earth has been a burning question for almost as long as humankind could look at the stars.

036 The controversy of the presidential election of 1860, one of the most important elections in American history, was associated with slavery; who would be given the power to change history was in the hands of the voters.

037 With all things prepared, when construction of the new housing areas begins depends on how soon the company reaches an agreement with local residents.

038 When an IQ test is scored, how the test taker's score compares to the standard deviation or average scores of all test takers is the main focus.

*standard deviation 표준 편차 ((통계 집단의 분배 정도를 나타내는 수치))

039 When evaluating a job opportunity, how much variety there is in the tasks you will perform is just as important as the salary and workload.

040 The best rocket launch sites tend to be remote, tropical locations. That such places are also often among the world's poorest gives many launches a counterintuitive feel: billions of dollars in futuristic machinery rising up over rainforests and shanty towns. ㅡ경찰대응용

*shanty 판잣집

QUESTION▶ 위 문장에서 밑줄 친 a counterintuitive feel이 의미하는 바로 적절한 것을 고르시오.
① Rocket launch sites are usually in wealthy areas, due to their access to high-technology.
② High-technology events like rocket launches are often located in areas that are undeveloped.

GOLDEN SAYING

To accomplish great things,
we must not only act,
but also dream; not only plan,
but also believe.

-Anatole France ((프랑스 소설가))

위대한 것을 성취하기 위해서, 우리는 행동해야 할 뿐 아니라,
또한 꿈을 꿔야 한다. 계획을 세울 뿐만 아니라, 또한 믿어야 한다.

CHAPTER 02

수식어구 뒤의 동사 찾기

Chapter Overview

- 주어와 동사 사이의 수식어(구, 절)가 있으면 주로 앞의 주어를 수식하는 형용사적 역할을 한다. 주어와 동사 사이가 떨어져서 동사를 찾기가 어려울 수 있지만 독해 지문에서 매우 흔하게 볼 수 있는 문장 구조이다.

- 수식어는 여러 개 겹쳐 올 수 있으므로 길이가 얼마든지 길어질 수 있다. 이와 같은 구조로 이해에 어려움을 주는 것들을 이번 챕터를 통해 말끔히 해결해본다.

Chapter Goals

1 주어를 뒤에서 수식할 수 있는 수식어구[절]를 열거할 수 있다.

2 주어 뒤에 온 수식어구[절]의 범위를 판단하여 동사를 파악할 수 있다.

Must-know
Words &
Lexical
Phrases

UNIT 05 •

041 proponent 지지자 (↔opponent 반대자); (논쟁 등의) 상대); 제안자

    thin (근거 등이) 빈약한, 불충분한; 여윈; 얇은

042 fluency 유창(함); 능란함

    cf. fluent 유창한; 능란한

    conscious 의식적인, 의도적인; 의식하는, 지각 있는

    cf. consciousness 의식; 자각

043 trigger 촉발하다; 계기; 방아쇠

    break down 분해하다, 부수다

    mass 질량

044 knowledgeable 아는 것이 많은; 총명한

    committed 헌신적인, 열성적인 (=dedicated, devoted)

    unconcerned 무관심한, 흥미 없는 (=indifferent)

045 contribute to A A의 원인이 되다; A에 기여하다

    interfere with ~을 방해하다, 훼방하다

    cf. interference 방해; 간섭, 참견

046 take A for granted A를 당연하게 여기다

    fair and square 정정당당한

048 interpretation 해석, 설명; 통역

    cf. interpret 해석하다, 설명하다; 통역하다

    threaten 조짐을 보이다; 위협하다, 협박하다

049 enthusiasm 열정, 열의

    cf. enthusiastic 열정적인, 열광하는

050 high-tech 첨단 기술의, 최첨단의

    authority 권위; 권한

    reliable 믿을 수 있는 (=dependable)

UNIT 06 •

051 literacy (글을) 읽고 쓸 줄 아는 능력 (↔illiteracy 문맹)

    cf. literate (글을) 읽고 쓸 줄 아는 (↔illiterate 문맹의)

    focal 중심의, 초점의

    cf. focal point 중점, 초점

    be at an advantage 유리한 위치에 있다

052 **beneficial** 유익한, 이로운

range from A to B (범위가) A에서 B까지 이르다

chronic 만성적인 (↔acute 급성의)

cf. **chronic disease** 만성 질환 ((오랜 기간 재발하는 질환))

053 **appropriate (for)** (~에) 적절한

054 **perseverance** 인내(심)

cf. **persevere** 인내하다; (끝까지) 해내다

capacity 능력; 용량, 수용력

humble 초라한, 미천한; 겸손한

056 **overland** 육로의, 육상의

overflow 넘치다; 초과; 범람

057 **self-respect** 자존감, 자존심

recall 떠올리다, 기억해내다 (=recollect)

058 **extract** 추출하다, 얻다; 발췌하다; 추출물

complex 복합적인; 복잡한; 합성물

cf. **complexity** 복잡성, 복잡함

mastery 숙달, 통달

059 **exhibit** (감정, 특징 등을) 보이다; 전시하다

060 **make up** 구성하다, 형성하다; 만들어 내다; 보상하다

061 **precision** 정밀(성), 정확(성) (=accuracy); 신중함

cf. **precise** 정확한, 정밀한

consistency 일관성; 농도

cf. **consistent** 일관된, 한결같은

grid (가로세로로) 격자무늬

apparent 식별할 수 있는, 또렷한; 분명한; 겉으로 보이는

aura 기운, 분위기

UNIT 07

063 **be unaware of** ~을 알지 못하다 (↔be aware of ~을 알다)

outlook 관점, 견해; 전망

064 **disastrous** 파멸을 초래하는; 처참한, 형편없는

(=catastrophic, devastating)

065 **stimulate** 장려하다, 활발하게 하다, 자극하다

involvement 몰입, 열중; 관여, 개입

066 **be capable of** ~을 할 수 있다; 유능하다

067 **unaided** 도움을 받지 않는

cf. **with the unaided eye** 맨눈으로 (=with the naked eye)

glow 불빛; 빛나다

galaxy 은하(계); ((the G-)) (태양계가 속한) 은하수

(=the Milky Way)

068 **strain** 피로, 긴장

itch 가렵다; 가려움

069 **sterilize** 살균하다, 소독하다

cf. **sterile** 소독한; 척박한; 불임의

072 **be composed of** ~로 구성되다 (=consist of)

UNIT 08 •

075 **molecule** ((화학)) 분자

cf. **molecular** 분자의

076 **proficiency** 능력, 능숙(도)

cf. **proficient** 능숙한

context 문맥; 맥락, 전후 사정

077 **firsthand** 직접(의)

cf. **secondhand** 간접(의); 중고의

to a[an] ~ extent ~한 정도로

cf. **to a great extent** 크게, 대부분은

078 **federal** 연방(정부)의

executive 행정관[부]; 경영 간부, 경영진; 경영의

079 **yield** 내다, 생산하다; 항복하다; 양보하다

080 **lead A to-v** A가 v하도록 이끌다

082 **inefficient** 비효율적인 (↔efficient 효율적인)

free up ~을 풀어주다, 해방하다

direct 향하다; 지시하다; 직접적인

innovative 혁신적인, 획기적인

cf. **innovate** 혁신하다

thrive 번영하다, 잘 자라다 (=flourish, prosper)

era 시대

084 **be aimed at** ~을 대상으로 하다, ~을 겨냥하다

outlaw 금지하다 (=ban)

call for ~을 요구하다

UNIT 05 주어 뒤 수식어구의 여러 형태

041 Proponents of the government economic policy argue the policy has played a central role in the country's economic success, when the evidence to support this is thin.

QUESTION 위 문장을 크게 두 개의 절로 나누고, 각 절의 주어를 수식하는 어구에 밑줄을 그으시오.

 Basic Points 영어에서 명사를 수식하는 수식어구[절]가 명사 뒤에 위치하는 것은 매우 흔한 구조이다. 그러나 우리말과는 어순이 다르고 수식어구의 형태가 여러 가지여서 익숙해지기 전에는 이해가 어렵기도 하다.

명사 뒤에 위치하는 대표적인 수식어구의 형태는 다음과 같다.

주어+수식어구+동사 ~
1. 전명구
2. 준동사구: to-v, v-ing, p.p.
3. 관계사절
4. 〈형용사+전명구〉
5. 동격어구[절](◁ Unit 38): of+명사, to-v, that절 (수식 역할은 아니지만 편의상 같이 다루기로 한다.)

042 Younger people learning a foreign language typically achieve fluency more easily than older learners, but there are many successful adult learners learning a language through conscious effort.

043 Triggered by low blood calcium levels, cells called osteoclasts break down bone to release calcium into the blood, potentially causing bone mass reduction. ─사관학교

*osteoclasts 파골세포 ((불필요한 뼈조직을 파괴하거나 흡수하는 세포))

044 Organizations built on knowledgeable and ⎡committed / unconcerned⎤ communities of users often find that good ideas come from the membership base who will also provide rapid feedback on whether a new service will work.

QUESTION 위 문장의 네모 안에서 문맥에 맞는 낱말로 적절한 것을 고르시오.

045 Anything that contributes to stress during mealtime can interfere with the digestion of food. ─수능

046 When we read advertisements, we usually take it for granted that any comparisons which they make to rival companies are not necessarily fair and square. −EBS 응용

047 Countries where sleep time has declined most dramatically over the past century are also those suffering the greatest increase in rates of physical diseases and mental disorders. −모의응용

048 In *The Interpretation of Dreams*, published in 1900, Sigmund Freud suggested that dreams occur when feelings and ideas unacceptable to the individual threaten / threatens to disturb sleep.

QUESTION▶ 위 문장의 네모 안에서 어법상 적절한 표현을 고르시오.

049 The ability to go from one failure to another without losing enthusiasm will bring you success.

050 The fact that information is conveyed in a high-tech manner somehow adds authority to what is conveyed, when in fact the Internet is a global conveyer of unfiltered, unedited, untreated information. −수능응용

TOPIC▶ the often reliable / misunderstood truth about information on the Internet

051 For many children, their first experiences with print occur in the home. Children from families that make literacy development a focal point of home activities via shared reading are at an advantage. —사관학교

QUESTION 두 번째 문장의 동사에 밑줄을 긋고, 동사의 수를 결정하는 주어에 동그라미 표시하시오.

🖋 **Main Points** 주어 뒤의 수식어구가 절을 포함할 때 길어질 수 있다. 수식어구 전체를 괄호로 묶어 주어와 동사가 한 눈에 보이도록 해보자.

052 The beneficial effects of regular exercise or physical activity range from fighting depression to reducing the risk of many chronic diseases such as heart disease and cancer.

QUESTION 위 문장의 동사에 밑줄을 그으시오.

053 The topics that people find amusing, and the occasions that are regarded as appropriate for joking, can vary enormously from one society to the next. —모의

QUESTION 위 문장의 동사에 밑줄을 그으시오.

✳ **Advanced Points** 수식어구에 and, or 등으로 나열되는 어구가 포함되면 범위를 파악하기가 더 어려울 수 있다. 또한 수식어구가 딸린 주어가 다른 주어와 나열될 때도 마찬가지다. 동사가 아직 나오지 않았는데 콤마(,)나 and가 보일 때는 그것이 연결하는 어구를 정확히 파악하고 문장 전체의 동사를 찾아야 한다.

054 With the power of hard work and perseverance, one's capacity to fight for what they want to achieve in life from its humble beginning creates their own destiny.

055 A number of people living in a country where they have to speak a foreign language [face / faces] social and practical challenges such as the language barrier.

QUESTION 위 문장의 네모 안에서 어법상 적절한 표현을 고르시오.

056 The loss or damage caused by overland flooding, which occurs when bodies of fresh water, such as rivers or dams overflow onto dry land, is partially covered by insurance companies.

057 One major difference between people with a low level of self-respect and those with a high level is the type of memories they choose to recall. −모의

058 People who extract the key ideas from new material, organize them into a mental model and connect that model to prior knowledge show an advantage in learning complex mastery. −경찰대

059 The exact influence of culture will differ from person to person, as no two individuals from the same country, region, religion, socio-economic class, gender, or generation will exhibit the same / different constellation of cultural behaviors and attitudes.

*socio-economic 사회 경제적인
**constellation (비슷한 것들의) 집합체, 모임

QUESTION 위 문장의 네모 안에서 문맥에 맞는 낱말로 적절한 것을 고르시오.

060 Places as unique and diverse as the wilds of East Africa's Serengeti, the Pyramids of Egypt, and the Great Barrier Reef in Australia make up our world's heritage.

*Great Barrier Reef 그레이트 배리어 리프 ((호주 해안의 세계 최대 산호초))

061 The precision of the lines, the consistency with which symbols are used, the grid and/or projection system, the apparent certainty with which place names are written, and the legend and scale information all give the map an aura of scientific accuracy and objectivity. −수능응용

*projection 투영(법) ((지구 표면을 오차 없이 평면으로 나타내는 방법))
**legend 지도의 범례 ((사용된 기호를 설명하는 부분))

QUESTION 위 문장의 동사에 밑줄을 그으시오.

062 Wise men and women in every major culture throughout history have found that the secret to happiness is not in getting more but in wanting less.

QUESTION 위 문장에서 주절의 동사에 밑줄을 그으시오.

🖋 **Main Points** 주어와 동사 사이의 수식어(구,절)는 여러 형태의 것이 연이어 나와 길어질 수도 있다. 순서대로 의미를 끊어서 이해하다가 동사가 나오면 수식어 부분 전체를 묶고 주어와 동사를 파악해보자.

063 The one benefit ① of jogging 30 minutes daily ② that most people are totally unaware of is that people who jog have a better outlook on life and are mentally a lot healthier.

QUESTION 위 문장에서 밑줄 친 ①, ②가 수식하는 것에 동그라미 표시하시오.

✳ **Advanced Points** 주어와 동사 사이의 여러 수식어구가 모두 주어를 수식하는 경우도 있다.

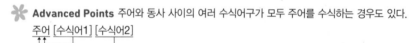

형용사구[절]가 무조건 바로 앞의 명사를 수식한다고 생각하면 문장의 의미를 잘 이해하지 못할 수도 있다. 문맥을 잘 살펴서 어떤 명사를 수식하는지를 정확히 판단해야 한다.

064 The idea of achieving security through national armament is, at the present state of military technique, a disastrous illusion. — Albert Einstein ((아인슈타인))

*armament 군비 (확충); 병기

065 The crucial factor in choosing literary works for foreign language learning is not just to select the appropriate level of language but to find works that stimulate the readers' involvement. — 경찰대응용

TOPIC the requirements / outcomes of effectively using literature for language learning

066 The skills required for making rational decisions amidst the complexities of free market economies are beyond the abilities of most consumers.

*amidst ~ 속에서, ~ 가운데에

QUESTION 위 문장에서 밑줄 친 beyond the abilities of most consumers가 의미하는 바로 적절한 것을 고르시오.
① Most consumers aren't capable of making rational decisions in free market economies.
② Making rational decisions in complex economies is a basic ability.

067 In a natural night sky, someone looking at the heavens with the unaided eye should be able to see nearly 3,500 stars and planets and the glow from the Milky Way, our home galaxy. −모의

068 One of the most common problems associated with overuse of a computer is eye strain, a common and annoying condition including tired, itching, and burning eyes. −모의응용

069 Pine seedlings grown in pots of soil sterilized by humans die within two or three years of being planted in the ground.

*seedling 묘목

070 Clothing appropriate for the temperature and environmental conditions in which you will be doing exercise can improve your exercise experience.

−모의응용

071 In the 1990s, the extension of patent laws as the only intellectual property rights tool into the area of seed varieties started to create a growing market for private seed companies. −수능

*intellectual property rights 지적 재산권

072 Teams working on a collaborative task that is / are composed of people with different personalities are more productive than teams composed of more similar individuals.

QUESTION▶ 위 문장의 네모 안에서 어법상 적절한 표현을 고르시오.

073 All of the women whom I have interviewed whose mothers worked said that they too would work when they had children. −사관학교응용

QUESTION▶ 위 문장의 동사에 밑줄을 그으시오.

074 Consider / Considering how I can make the world a better place for another person shows my love for others and pulls me out of myself, lifting my thoughts to a grander place. – 모의응용

QUESTION 위 문장의 네모 안에서 어법상 적절한 표현을 고르시오.

🖋 **Main Points** Unit 01부터 Unit 07까지 학습한 내용을 바탕으로, 어법 문제로 많이 출제되는 포인트인 동사/준동사 자리에 대해 알아보자. 동사는 주어의 동작이나 상태를 서술하고, 준동사는 문장에서 주어, 목적어, 보어, 수식어 역할을 한다.

절에는 주어와 동사가 있고 절과 절의 연결은 접속사나 관계사로 하므로, 접속사[관계사] 없이 한 문장에 두 개의 동사가 있을 수 없다. 동사가 두 개 있으려면 접속사나 관계사가 한 개 더 있어야 한다.
동사의 개수 = 접속사[관계사]의 개수+1

075 Since the human body is basically an extremely complex system of interacting molecules, the technology required to truly understand and repair the body is molecular machine technology.

QUESTION 위 문장에서 주절의 동사에 밑줄을 그으시오.

✳ **Error Points** 동사가 과거형과 과거분사(p.p.)가 같은 형태이면 혼동을 줄 수 있다. 특히 주어 다음에 p.p.가 동사보다 먼저 나오면 동사로 착각하기 쉬우므로, 늘 주의해야 한다.
The man **injured** in the accident **was taken** to hospital. 사고로 **부상당한** 그 사람이 병원에 **실려갔다.**
　　　　　　과거분사(p.p.)　　　　　　　　　　　동사

076 To improve your reading proficiency, learning to consider the subject of the reading material and make guesses about the context is essential.

077 Because it would be impossible for you to discover huge stores of historical or scientific evidence firsthand, studying in high school and college, to a great extent, depends / depending on reading books and other documents.

QUESTION 위 문장의 네모 안에서 어법상 적절한 표현을 고르시오.

078 Certain kinds of specialized professionals, such as scientists and engineers, <u>worked</u> for the federal government express much less satisfaction with their work than federal executives. – 경찰대

QUESTION 위 문장의 밑줄 친 부분이 어법상 올바르면 ○표, 틀리면 ✕표 하고 바르게 고치시오.

079 Computers may yield important predictions about complex phenomena, but the predictions they make can never be relied on without experimental confirmation. −모의

080 A clear understanding of what your purpose is in life leads you to do whatever is necessary to achieve it.

081 Feelings and judgments about how others feel toward you <u>playing</u> a major role in how you choose to solve your day-to-day problems. −수능응용

QUESTION▶ 위 문장의 밑줄 친 부분이 어법상 올바르면 ○표, 틀리면 ✕표 하고 바르게 고치시오.

082 Those countries that are most willing to let capitalism quickly destroy inefficient companies, so that money can be freed up and directed to more innovative ones, thriving / will thrive in the era of globalization. −사관학교응용

QUESTION▶ 위 문장의 네모 안에서 어법상 적절한 표현을 고르시오.

083 Knowledge gained through workplace experience <u>is</u> far more important than grades earned in school in predicting the job performance of new employees.

QUESTION▶ 위 문장의 밑줄 친 부분이 어법상 올바르면 ○표, 틀리면 ✕표 하고 바르게 고치시오.

084 Television advertising of products aimed at children under 12 has been outlawed by the Swedish government and, in the United States, 50 psychologists signed a petition calling for a ban on the advertising of children's goods. −모의응용

*petition 청원(서)

GOLDEN SAYING

The depth of darkness to which
you can descend and still live is
an exact measure of the height
to which you can aspire to reach.

-Pliny the Elder ((고대 로마 정치인))

당신이 내려가 여전히 살아있을 수 있는 어둠의 깊이가,
당신이 닿고자 열망할 수 있는 높이의 정확한 척도다.
(절망이 깊은 만큼 높이 솟을 수 있다.)

03

명사 뒤 수식어구로 인한 문제들

Chapter Overview

● 뒤에 오는 수식어구로 인한 독해의 걸림돌은 주어가 아닌 다른 명사들 뒤에서도 똑같이 나타날 수 있다.

● 주어 뒤의 수식어구는 문장의 동사 직전까지로 생각하면 되지만, 주어가 아닌 명사(목적어, 보어, 전치사의 목적어)의 수식어구는 그 범위를 착각하게 되는 경우가 많아 좀 더 어려울 수 있다. 어디부터 어디까지가 어느 명사에 대한 수식어구인지를 정확히 판단할 수 있어야 해석도 정확하게 할 수 있다.

Chapter Goals

1 문장에서 〈명사+수식어구〉로 이루어진 부분을 찾아 명사가 문장에서 어떤 역할을 하는지 말할 수 있다.

2 목적격보어의 다양한 형태를 나열할 수 있다.

3 〈목적어(+수식어구 등)+목적격보어〉로 이루어진 문장에서 목적격보어의 위치를 알 수 있다.

4 여러 수식어구가 겹쳐서 올 때 각 수식어구가 어떤 명사를 수식하는지 알 수 있다.

Must-know
Words &
Lexical
Phrases

UNIT 09 •

085 boost 고양, 북돋움, 격려; 북돋우다

　　self-esteem 자존감, 자부심

086 serve a purpose 사용되다; 도움이 되다

087 mere 단순한, 순전한, 단지 ~에 불과한

　　cf. **merely** 단지, 한낱, 그저

　　mobility 이동성, 유동성

　　cf. **upward mobility** 사회적[경제적] 상승

　　sole 유일한; 혼자의; (신발의) 밑창

　　determinant 결정 요인

　　cf. **determine** 결정하다; 알아내다, 밝히다

　　attain 얻다, 획득하다; 이루다

　　escalate 증가되다; 확대시키다

　　unobserved 눈에 띄지 않는

088 applicant 지원자

　　cf. **apply** 지원하다

　　　application 적용(성); 신청(서), 지원(서)

　　hardship 어려움, 곤란

091 destined ~할 운명인; ~행(行)의

　　old-fashioned 구식의, 유행이 지난

　　preserve 보존하다; 보호하다 (=conserve)

　　extinct 멸종된

092 implicit 암묵적인, 내포된 (↔explicit 분명한, 명백한); 절대적인

093 splendid 눈부신, 뛰어난; 화려한

　　cf. **splendor** 훌륭함, 화려함

094 depict 묘사하다 (=describe); (그림으로) 그리다

　　engage in ~에 몰두하다, 종사하다

　　cf. **engage** 끌어들이다; (주의, 관심을) 사로잡다

　　　engaging 매력 있는

　　instant 즉각적인, 즉시의 (=immediate)

UNIT 10 •

095 migrate 이주[이동]하다

　　cf. **migration** 이주, 이동

　　agent 행위자; 대리인; 요인, 동인

096 **maximize** 극대화하다

　　seek out 찾아내다

097 **radical** 근본적인; 급진적인

099 **result from** ～에서 비롯되다, ～이 원인이다

　　cf. **result in** (결과적으로) ～을 낳다

　　assertiveness 자기주장

　　cf. **assertive** 단정적인, 주장하는; 확신에 찬

　　mandatory 의무적인, 필수의 (＝compulsory)

　　cf. **mandate** 명령(하다); 위임(하다); 권한

100 **distrust** 불신하다; 불신(감)

　　ambivalent 양면적인, 반대 감정이 공존하는

101 **get there** (목표 등을) 달성하다

　　worthwhile 가치 있는

　　cf. **be worthwhile to-v** v할 가치가 있다

102 **retention** 기억(력); 유지, 보유; 정체

　　cf. **retain** 잊지 않고 있다; 유지하다, 보유하다

104 **detrimental** 해로운 (＝harmful)

U N I T **1 1** •

105 **promote** 진척시키다; 홍보하다; 승진시키다

　　staff (주로 수동태로) 직원으로 일하다; 직원

　　carry out 수행하다

　　turn A into B A를 B로 바꾸다

106 **indicate** 보여주다, 나타내다

　　psychological 정신적인, 정신의

　　trauma 정신적 충격

107 **cruelty** 잔인함; 학대

　　laboratory 실험실

110 **derive A from B** B에서 A를 얻다

　　photosynthesize 광합성을 하다

　　cf. **photosynthesis** 광합성

　　sustainable 지속 가능한

　　renewable 재생 가능한

112 **trait** (성격상의) 특성, 속성 (＝characteristic, feature)

　　magnificent 훌륭한, 매우 감명 깊은

113 **alliance** 동맹; 동맹 단체

　　cf. **ally** 동맹시키다; 동맹국

　　sophisticated 정교한; 세련된

　　apart from ～을 제외하고; ～ 외에도

114 **temptation** 유혹

U N I T **1 2** •

115 **adolescence** 청소년기

　　cf. **adolescent** 청소년

　　go through ～을 겪다[경험하다]; ～을 조사하다

116 **lengthy** 장황한, 너무 긴; 지루한

117 **afford** (시간, 금전적) 여유가 되다; 제공하다

　　cf. **can[can't] afford to-v** v할 여유가 되다[안 되다]

　　relieve 완화하다; 안심시키다; (고통 등을) 덜다

118 **strive** 노력하다, 분투하다

119 **psycholinguistic** 심리 언어학의

　　awareness 인식, 자각

　　facet 측면, 양상

　　read between the lines 행간을 읽다, 숨겨진 의미를 파악하다

　　infer 추론하다; 암시하다

　　bias 성향; 편견; 선입견을 품게 하다

120 **impotent** 무능한, 무력한 (↔potent 강력한)

　　go about (문제 등을) 다루다; ～하고 다니다

　　possessed (생각 따위에) 사로잡힌

121 **take time out** 시간을 내다

122 **in place of** ～을 대신하여

123 **cannot help v-ing** v하지 않을 수 없다

　　look on A as B A를 B라고 여기다

124 **assumption** 가정, 추정; (권력, 책임의) 인수, 장악

125 **genetically modified** 유전자 변형의

UNIT 09 명사 수식어 자리

085 Some experts declare many reasons why all people — young and old — have to do some volunteer work: it can provide a healthy boost to your self-confidence, self-esteem, and life satisfaction.

QUESTION 위 문장에서 〈명사+수식어구〉로 이루어진 부분을 찾아 명사에 밑줄을 긋고, 그 역할이 주어, 보어, 목적어 중 어느 것인지 쓰시오.

Ⅴ **Basic Points** 문장에서 주어 외에 명사가 올 수 있는 자리는 목적어(O) 또는 명사 보어(C)로, 각각 수식어가 따를 수 있다.
S+V+C(+M)
S+V+O(+M)
S+V+O(+M)+O(+M)
S+V+O(+M)+C(+M)

문장의 동사 외에 준동사의 목적어나 명사 보어도 수식을 받을 수 있고, 전치사의 목적어인 명사 또한 수식을 받을 수 있다.

086 The scents of plants or fruits can serve various purposes; lavender can fill you with feelings of tranquility, and peppermint is one of the best scents to improve concentration and memory.

*tranquility 평온

087 Education and "know-how" are no longer mere keys to upward social mobility; they are now the sole determinants of whether a person will attain success and financial power.

TOPIC the escalating / unobserved importance of learning and knowledge

088 During the job interview, the interviewer asked the applicant a personal question about their greatest hardship.

089 The English consider good manners an essential skill to learn in school as well as at home.

090 We hope that stem cell research and technology will help us to cure or prevent many of the illnesses that kill millions today. *stem cell 줄기세포

091 One may wonder if literary fiction is destined to become an old-fashioned genre to be preserved in a museum like an existing / extinct species. –수능

> **QUESTION** 위 문장의 네모 안에서 문맥에 맞는 낱말로 적절한 것을 고르시오.

092 Some cultures maintain an implicit "schedule" for <u>the right time</u> to do many important things; for example, the right time to start dating, to finish college, to buy your own home, or to have a child. –모의응용

> **QUESTION** 위 문장에서 밑줄 친 <u>the right time</u>이 의미하는 바로 적절한 것을 고르시오.
> ① the time that is considered socially desirable
> ② the time people achieve their goals earlier than their rivals

093 People with bluebird syndrome are not satisfied with their life, and may dream about a splendid future waiting for them, but do not put any effort into trying to create that future.

094 Certainly, the images of success depicted in the media rarely show the years of struggle and practice that musicians, actors, or athletes engage in before their "instant" successes. –모의응용

> **SUMMARY** The media pay little / much attention to the time and effort that success requires.

목적어 뒤의 목적격보어 찾기

095 Just as we <u>consider</u> the people who migrated to the new place active agents of some change, we must also consider the role played by the migration of plants, animals, and germs.

QUESTION 위 문장에서 밑줄 친 <u>consider</u>의 목적격보어를 찾아 밑줄을 그으시오.

096 Maximizing the power of positive influence by seeking out people you can respect and admire is a good way <u>to have</u> your dreams, goals, and ambitions come true.

QUESTION 위 문장에서 밑줄 친 <u>to have</u>의 목적격보어를 찾아 밑줄을 그으시오.

🌱 **Main Points** SVOC 문형에서 목적어(O) 뒤에 수식어구가 오면 목적격보어(C)와 서로 떨어지게 되므로 주의해야 한다. 목적어와 목적격보어 사이에 삽입어구가 있거나, 목적어가 나열되어 길어질 때도 목적격보어를 찾기 어려울 수 있다.

SVOC 문형에서 목적어 뒤에 오는 C의 형태는 다음과 같다.
- SVO<u>C(명사)</u>: C는 O의 직위, 직업, 이름 등의 신분 (O=C)
- SVO<u>C(형용사)</u>: C는 O의 성질, 상태 등
- SVO<u>C(to-v, v, v-ing)</u>: C는 O가 하는 동작
- SVO<u>C(p.p.)</u>: C는 O가 당하는 동작

097 The "knowledge society" represents a radical change, because it enables new forms of knowledge socialization and new possibilities to store the output of learning across time and space. −EBS 응용

✳ **Error Points** SVO 문형의 목적어 뒤에 오는 부분이 목적격보어가 아니라 목적어의 수식어일 수도 있기 때문에 문맥에 맞게 판단하여 SVOC 문형으로 오역하지 않도록 주의하자. SVOC 문형의 목적어(O)와 목적격보어(C) 사이에는 반드시 주어와 술어의 관계(O가 C하다)가 성립한다.

098 Most instructors and learners find active instructional strategies, such as group projects, more engaging, while some find factors such as time pressure obstacles to active learning.

099 Because of dangerous incidents that resulted from poor communication, the Federal Aviation Administration made assertiveness training for all airline crew members mandatory to ensure they have the ability to communicate effectively. – 경찰대응용

*Federal Aviation Administration 미국 연방항공국

100 The public has come to expect the steady increase in the standard of living that new developments in science and technology have brought **to continue**, but it also distrusts science because it has no clear understanding of science. – 경찰대응용

TOPIC the ⟨ambivalent / trustful⟩ attitude of the public toward science

101 Leaders seek a vision for an organization and sell that vision in such a way that the desired goal makes the effort of getting there seem worthwhile.

102 We let most of the facts and data we face everyday pass through our brains with minimal retention or reaction — unless we take special care to retain the information. – 모의응용

103 Exciting live shows and street performances by various movie characters got the whole crowd in the theme park cheering and wanting for more.

104 Having too many options can be _____ to our happiness. Because we can't remove the rejected choices from our minds, we experience the disappointment of having our satisfaction with decisions reduced by all the options we did not choose. – 모의응용

FILL-IN ① beneficial   ② detrimental

Plus⁺ SVOO 문형에서 두 목적어 사이가 떨어지는 경우

SVOO 문형의 경우에도 먼저 나오는 간접목적어(IO)가 전명구, to부정사구, 분사구, 관계사절 등의 수식을 받아 길어질 때, 두 번째 목적어인 직접목적어(DO)를 찾기 어려울 수 있으므로 주의해야 한다.

The teacher regularly <u>assigns</u> **students** (in online courses) **a quiz** (of thirty objective questions).
　　　　　　　　　　V　　　　　IO　　　　　　　　　　　　　　DO

그 선생님은 온라인 수업을 듣는 학생들에게 객관식 30개 문제 시험을 정기적으로 낸다.

The school clinic staff <u>notified</u> **parents** [whose children had severe cavities] **that they should schedule**
　　　　　　　　　　　　　V　　　　IO　　　　　　　　　　　　　　　　　　　　　　　DO(that절)
appointments with a local dentist.

학교 양호실 직원은 충치가 심각한 아이들의 부모에게 동네 치과 예약을 잡아야 한다고 알렸다.

105 Renaissance artists who promoted the idea of creative genius operated workshops ① staffed by artist assistants ② who carried out most of the labor involved in turning their master's design into a work of art. – 사관학교응용

QUESTION ▶ 위 문장에서 밑줄 친 ①, ②가 각각 수식하는 명사에 동그라미 표시하시오.

🖋 **Main Points** 명사를 수식하는 형용사구나 관계사절은 둘 이상이 연달아 올 수도 있는데, 대개는 바로 앞의 명사를 수식한다.
명사 [수식어구1] [수식어구2] [수식어구3] ~

106 Researchers have found evidence ① of long-lasting damage ② indicating that psychological trauma physically affects the brain.

QUESTION ▶ 위 문장에서 밑줄 친 ①, ②가 각각 수식하는 명사에 동그라미 표시하시오.

✳ **Advanced Points** 하나의 명사를 두 개 이상의 형용사구나 관계사절이 수식할 수도 있다. 바로 앞의 명사를 수식하는 문맥이 어색하면 좀 더 앞의 명사를 수식하는 것이 아닌지를 살펴봐야 한다.
명사 [수식어구1] [수식어구2] ~

관계사절이 두 개 이상 이어질 때 등위접속사 and 등으로 연결되기도 한다. (≪ Unit 25 병렬구조)

107 Since the 1960s, animal rights groups around the world have tried to make people aware of the cruelty affecting animals used for laboratory research.

108 Much of your e-mail comes from complete strangers who don't know you and who just want to sell you something you probably don't really want.

109 In Ancient Rome, messages sent over short distances, for which a quick reply was expected, were written with a stylus on wax tablets that folded together like a book. – 사관학교응용

*stylus 철필 **wax tablet 납판 ((고대의 필기장))

110 _____ there are more and more examples of positive practices relying on bio-energy (energy derived from photosynthesizing organisms) that can be brought to larger scale, we have hardly begun to build a sustainable and renewable bio-based economy.

FILL-IN ① While ② Because

111 Not all interesting discoveries have an obvious application, which is why there were many innovations that were matched to a product which languished in labs for years. −모의응용

*languish 유보되다, 미루어지다

112 The one trait of heroes who are truly magnificent that goes beyond all cultural boundaries is the willingness to risk one's life for the good of others.

−사관학교응용

113 Researchers who have spent thousands of hours observing the behavior of bottlenose dolphins have discovered that the males form social alliances with one another that are far more sophisticated than any alliance which is seen in animals apart from human beings. −경찰대응용

*bottlenose dolphins 큰돌고래

QUESTION 위 문장에서 수컷 큰돌고래에 대한 내용과 일치하는 것을 고르시오.
① 인간과 동일한 수준으로 정교한 사회적 동맹을 맺는다.
② 인간을 제외한 동물들 사이에서 가장 정교한 사회적 동맹을 맺는다.

114 When a counselor's client seeks information regarding the direction he or she should take, like what choice to make or what approach to use, there is ever present a strong temptation on the counselor's part to tell him or her what to do, which is avoided to allow clients to make independent decisions.

수식어구의 범위

115 Adolescence is considered to be the time teenagers go through biological development, and, more importantly, form personal identities.

QUESTION 위 문장의 밑줄 친 the time을 수식하는 어구에 밑줄을 그으시오.

116 We often provide lengthy scientific explanations for children's questions, which can be much better answered with a picture that can make them imagine or a direct experience of something similar. —모의응용

QUESTION 위 문장의 밑줄 친 a picture을 수식하는 어구에 밑줄을 그으시오.

🖋 **Main Points** 명사를 수식하는 수식어구의 범위가 문장 끝까지 이어지는지 중간에 끝나는지를 잘 판단해야 한다.

117 The government introduced a new system to allow the poor to borrow money they couldn't afford to relieve their financial difficulties and social issues.

QUESTION 위 문장의 밑줄 친 money를 수식하는 어구에 밑줄을 그으시오.

✴ **Error Points** 수식어구의 범위 밖에 있는 어구를 수식어구에 포함되는 것으로 혼동하는 경우를 주의해야 한다. 위 예문의 경우, 〈can[could] afford to-v (v할 여유가 되다)〉 표현이 사용되었다고 생각하면 afford to relieve ~가 자연스럽게 이어지는 것 같지만 여기서 to relieve는 '목적(완화하기 위하여)'을 나타낸다.

118 We strive towards the day when nations will be judged not by their military or economic strength, nor by the splendor of their capital cities and public buildings, but by the well-being of their children. —UNICEF ((유니세프, 국제 연합 아동 기금))

*splendor 화려함

119 Reading is an incredibly complex psycholinguistic activity involving not only phonemic awareness and alphabet recognition, but also comprehension in all its facets — reading between the lines, inferring meaning, and detecting the author's bias. —경찰대응용

*phonemic (최소의 소리 단위인) 음소(音素)의

120 Anger is the most impotent of passions. It effects nothing it goes about, and hurts the one who is possessed by it more than the one against whom it is directed. – Carl Sandburg ((美 시인))

121 Take time out to do things that you enjoy after work in order to reduce the stress which you experience during your working hours.

122 Hardly any two words in a language have precisely the same meaning and usage; and we can seldom put a word in place of the one which a great writer has used without making a change for the worse. – 모의응용

> **QUESTION** 위 문장의 내용과 일치하는 것을 고르시오.
> ① 위대한 작가의 단어도 더 나은 것으로 바뀔 수 있다.
> ② 위대한 작가가 쓴 단어를 바꾸면 더 나쁜 쪽으로 바뀌기 쉽다.

123 I cannot help fearing that men may reach a point where they look on every new theory as a danger, every innovation as a toilsome trouble, every social advance as a first step toward revolution, and that they may absolutely refuse to move at all. – Alexis de Tocqueville ((프랑스 정치학자))   *toilsome 힘든, 고된

124 The enemy of "learning" is "knowing," since knowing means you won't see the assumptions that exist behind what you think and know, which means that the thinking process leading to knowing may never be revisited. – 모의응용

> **SUMMARY** Properly learning something requires | a lack of / a lot of | existing knowledge.

125 In a study of behavior toward genetically modified food, participants actually received the food options they chose to encourage truthful responding.

GOLDEN SAYING

If you let your fear of consequence
prevent you from following
your deepest instinct, your life
will be safe, expedient and thin.

-Katharine Butler Hathaway ((美 저술가))

결과에 대한 두려움이 당신의 가장 깊숙한 본능을 따라가지 못하게 한다면,
당신의 인생은 패기가 없고, 편리함만 추구하며, 얄팍할 것이다.

CHAPTER

04

문장 구조 파악을 어렵게 하는 것들

Chapter Overview

삽입절이나 수식어구의 위치, 형태적인 특징, 단어의 익숙하지 않은 쓰임 등으로 인해 문장 구조 파악이 어려운 경우에 대해 학습한다.

Chapter Goals

1 관계대명사절 내에 자주 삽입되는 절을 파악할 수 있다.

2 다양한 역할이 가능한 단어[어구]가 문장에서 어떻게 쓰였는지 정확히 판별할 수 있다.

3 문장 내 부사구[절]의 위치에 상관없이 문장 구조를 파악할 수 있다.

4 분사구문의 예외적인 형태를 파악할 수 있다.

Must-know Words & Lexical Phrases

UNIT13 •

126 turn to A A에 의존하다

127 substance 물질; 본질, 핵심

  cf. **substantial** 물질적인; 본질적인; 상당한

  cleanse 깨끗하게 하다, 정화하다

128 explosion 폭발적인 증가; 폭발

  knowledgeable 많이 아는

  condition 질병[질환]; 조건; 상태

129 reliable 신뢰할 만한, 믿을 수 있는 (=dependable)

130 assemble 조합하다, 모으다[모이다]; 조립하다

131 for A's own sake A 자체로

  immoral 비도덕적인 (↔moral 도덕적인)

132 absorb (정보를) 받아들이다; 흡수하다

  considerable 상당한

  relevance 관련(성); 적절, 타당성

133 disgusting 정말로 싫은; 역겨운, 구역질 나는

134 syllabus (강의 등의) 개요, 시간표

135 take A for granted A를 당연하다고 여기다

UNIT14 •

136 acquaintance 친분, 면식; 지인

  precondition 전제 조건

  document 뒷받침하다, 입증하다; 기록하다; 서류, 문서

137 justified 정당한

  cf. **justify** 정당화하다; 타당함을 보여주다

138 contract 수축하다; 계약하다; 계약

139 sequence 순서, 차례; 연달아 일어남, 연속

140 efficacy 효능; 유효

  cognitive 인지의, 인식의

141 just around the corner 이제 곧, 임박하여; 모퉁이를 돈 곳에

142 central 가장 중요한

143 converge (on) (한 곳에) 모이다, 집중되다; 모으다

144 indifferent 무관심한 (=apathetic)

  forgo 보류하다, 삼가다

  apathetic 무관심한

146 trillion 1조; 엄청난 양

habitable 거주하기에 적당한, 살기 알맞은

UNIT 15 •

147 the last word 결정적인 사실, 최종적 발언

148 priority 우선권

consideration 고려 사항; 사려, 숙고

cf. **take A into consideration** A를 고려하다

149 manifest (감정을) 표현하다, 드러내다; 나타나다; 명백한

gratitude 감사, 고마움

generosity 관대함; 너그러움

dedicate oneself to A A에 헌신하다

151 knock ~의 상태로 만들다; 두드리다, 부수다; 노크하다

off course 경로를 벗어난

setback 좌절; 패배; 방해

straightforward 간단한

dimension 차원; (공간의) 크기, 치수; 규모

cf. **multidimensional** 다차원의; 다양한

152 dependent (on) (~에) 좌우되는, 의존하는

153 bloodstream 혈류, 피의 흐름

supply A to B A를 B에게 제공하다 (=supply B with A)

154 advocate 지지자, 옹호자; 지지[옹호]하다

unhindered 제약[방해]을 받지 않는

cf. **hinder** 방해하다, 못하게 하다

intervention 간섭, 개입; 중재

cf. **intervene** 개입하다; 중재하다

yield 총수익; 생산(량); 생산하다, 산출하다

156 identify 확인하다, 알아보다; 동일시하다

cf. **identical** 똑같은, 동일한

preference 선호

overwhelmed 압도되는

clarify 분명히 하다

157 rage (폭풍 등이) 맹렬히 계속되다; 격노; 열정, 열망

cutting-edge 최첨단의

artificial 인공의

cf. **artificial intelligence** 인공 지능

pinpoint 정확히 찾아내다; 정확한

blaze (대형) 화재; 불길

UNIT 16 •

158 at hand 항상 사용할 수 있는; 가까이에

bilingual 2개 국어를 사용하는

occupational 직업과 관련된, 직업의

159 composition 구성(물); 작문; 작곡; (음악·미술·문학) 작품

narrative 이야기체의; 이야기, 설화

chronological 시간 순서대로 된, 연대순의

161 fulfill 실현시키다, 달성하다; 이행하다

162 note 음(조); 메모, 기록; 주목하다

163 antiquity 고대, 아주 오래됨; 유물

comprehensive 해박한, 이해력이 있는; 포괄적인, 종합적인

range over (다양한 주제를) 다루다[아우르다]

landscape 분야, ~계; 풍경

164 courtesy 친절, 정중한 행동[말]

come A's way A에게 (일이) 닥치다

uneasy 불안한

string ((복수형)) 조건; 끈, 줄; 일련

165 troublesome 골칫거리인

be accustomed to A A에 익숙해지다

indispensable 없어서는 안 될, 필수적인

(↔dispensable 없어도 되는, 불필요한)

167 moralist 윤리학자; 도덕주의자

cf. **morality** 윤리, 도덕

code 규범, 규칙; 암호, 부호

169 ongoing 계속 진행 중인

momentum 추진력; 계기; 운동량

persevere 인내하며 계속하다, 인내심을 가지고 하다

삽입절을 포함하는 관계사절

126 Some readers turn to history for adventure, and escape; others seek the lessons which they believe it will teach.

> **QUESTION** 위 문장에서 삽입절 부분을 ( )로 묶으시오.

> 🖋 **Main Points** 관계대명사 뒤에 〈주어+동사〉가 주로 앞뒤의 콤마(,) 없이 삽입되는 경우가 있다. 삽입된 〈주어+동사〉를 괄호로 묶어 보면 문장 구조를 좀 더 쉽게 파악할 수 있다.
> Other readers seek the lessons. + They believe (that) history will teach the lessons.
>
> Other readers seek *the lessons* **which (they believe)** history will teach ●.
> 다른 독자들은 **(그들이 믿기에)** 역사가 가르쳐 줄 교훈을 구한다.
>
> 삽입절은 원래 that절을 목적어절로 취하는 주절의 형태〈S+V+that ~〉에서 목적어절을 이끄는 that이 생략된 형태가 대부분이다. 삽입절로 자주 등장하는 예는 아래와 같으며 주로 부사적으로 해석하면 자연스럽다.
> • I believe[think, suppose]: 내가 믿기에[생각하기에]   • it seems (to me): (내가) 보기에
> • I'm sure[certain]: 내가 확신하는데   • they said: 그들의 말에 의하면

127 Believe it or not, the substance that we believe is cleansing us is actually hurting us by polluting our environment.

128 The information technology explosion has enabled patients to become much more knowledgeable about medical matters than they used to be, so sometimes they form firm views about the treatment that they think is appropriate for their condition. —모의응용

129 Not all sources of information are reliable, so you should evaluate all of your sources of information and use only those that you think are debatable / dependable .

> **QUESTION** 위 문장의 네모 안에서 문맥에 맞는 낱말로 적절한 것을 고르시오.

130 Many designers, working on a project, assemble images of the sort of people for whom the product is intended, the surroundings in which they suppose it will be used, and other products that the intended user group might own, seeking to capture the flavor of their life-style.

131 If we value diversity or the unusual for its own sake, we will be forced into valuing things which it seems we do not want to value — randomly creating odd species, or unusual, immoral practices only because they are diverse.

132 A recent study shows that aging does not affect the amount of information that you expect you can absorb in a given period. And once you've learned it, you'll probably retain it as well as a younger person does. −모의응용

SUMMARY Aging has considerable / little relevance to the ability to learn, according to a recent study.

133 With only few exceptions, my teenagers now love vegetables, which they used to say were disgusting, and so I include them in every meal.

134 You've probably had science and math classes in school, but not lessons on how to manage your money, which some might say is equally or more important than other subjects in the syllabus.

135 The simple act of eating, which most of us know is taken for granted, is a daily challenge for children with food allergies because even a small bite of an allergen could have tragic consequences.

*allergen 알레르기를 유발하는 물질

착각하기 쉬운 단어의 역할

136 Some contact or acquaintance between people is an essential precondition for the formation of a relationship. <u>Evidence</u> from some researchers documents the obvious fact that the less the physical distance, the more likely they are to develop social visiting relationships. —사관학교응용

QUESTION 위 문장에서 밑줄 친 주어 Evidence의 동사를 찾아 밑줄을 그으시오.

 Main Points 주로 명사로 쓰이는 단어들이 문장에서 동사로 쓰이거나, 주로 동사로 쓰이는 단어들이 명사로 쓰이면 문장 구조 파악이 어려울 수 있다. 단어나 어구는 여러 품사로 쓰일 수 있으며, 때로는 품사 고유의 형태와 다른 역할을 하는 경우도 있으므로 이에 주의해야 한다.

1. 명사/형용사로 잘 쓰이지만 동사로도 쓰이는 단어들
question, form, handle, function, complete, schedule, limit, matter, experience, approach, access, cost, contract, concern, challenge, finance, implement 등

2. 동사로 잘 쓰이지만 명사로도 쓰이는 단어들
support, decline, must(필수품), might(힘), need(욕구) 등

3. 명사, 부사, 분사 형태의 접속사들
the moment[instant, minute]: ~하자마자　　　　every[each] time: ~할 때마다 (= whenever)
(just) the way: ~처럼　　　　　　　　　　　　once: ~하자마자; 일단 ~하면
now (that): ~이므로, ~이기 때문에　　　　　　given that : ~를 고려하면
seeing (that[as]): ~이므로, ~이라는 점에서 보면 (= because, considering that, in that)
provided (that), supposing[suppose] (that), assuming (that): 만약 ~라면 (= if)

4. v-ing 형태의 전치사: 명사를 수식하는 것으로 착각하지 않도록 한다.
considering: ~을 고려하면　　　　　　　　　including: ~을 포함하여
pending: ~을 기다리는 동안에　　　　　　　　regarding: ~에 관해서는 (= concerning, respecting)
excluding: ~을 제외하고 (= excepting)　　　　barring: ~이 없으면

5. 여러 형태의 부사들
put simply: 간단히 말하자면　　　　　　　　　no doubt: 분명[아마] ~일 것이다 (= probably, almost certainly)
to date: 지금까지 (= up to now, until today[now], so far)

137 Animal rights activists question whether research with animals is necessary for scientific and medical progress, and if all of the experiments and the animals used are justified and required.

138 When it is dry, the cactus contracts like an accordion to minimize the surface area exposed to the sun and retain as much water as possible. —모의　*cactus 선인장

139 In most Western cultures, messages usually concern ideas presented in a logical sequence. The speaker tries to say what is meant through precise wording, and the content of the language is more objective than personal.

QUESTION▶ 위 글에서 첫 번째 문장의 동사를 찾아 밑줄을 그으시오.

140 One study evaluated the efficacy of a daily multivitamin to prevent cognitive decline among 5,947 elderly males. −사관학교

QUESTION▶ 위 문장에서 밑줄 친 decline의 품사로 알맞은 것을 고르시오.
① 명사   ② 동사

141 Old age occurs the moment you realize there isn't something wonderful about to happen just around the corner.

142 Now that knowledge matters more than ever, higher education is central to the growth strategy of most countries.

143 The various religions are like different roads converging on the same point. What difference does it make if we follow different routes, provided we arrive at the same destination? −Mahatma Gandhi

144 Our species is so careless and indifferent not only to forgo action regarding the obvious environmental threats we face but to ignore them altogether.

SUMMARY▶ Humans are ⎡focused / apathetic⎤ on environmental issues.

145 In children, pairing foods with the presence of friends, a liked celebrity, or attention by adults all increases liking for those foods, no doubt reflecting the positive value of each of these groups to the children.

146 To date we know of at least 3,700 exoplanets and there are likely to be trillions of other potentially habitable exoplanets and exomoons in our galaxy and beyond. −경찰대

*exoplanet (태양계 밖의) 외계 행성 **exomoon 외계 위성

부사의 자유로운 위치

147 Audiences are encouraged by the media to accept their news reports as the last word on any particular topic or event.

QUESTION 위 문장에서 중간에 삽입된 부사구를 찾아 밑줄을 그으시오.

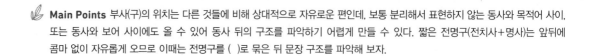

🌿 **Main Points** 부사(구)의 위치는 다른 것들에 비해 상대적으로 자유로운 편인데, 보통 분리해서 표현하지 않는 동사와 목적어 사이, 또는 동사와 보어 사이에도 올 수 있어 동사 뒤의 구조를 파악하기 어렵게 만들 수 있다. 짧은 전명구(전치사＋명사)는 앞뒤에 콤마 없이 자유롭게 오므로 이때는 전명구를 ( )로 묶은 뒤 문장 구조를 파악해 보자.

148 To stop being late, all one has to do is change the motivation by deciding <u>that</u> in all circumstances being on time is going to have first priority over any other consideration. －모의

QUESTION 위 문장의 밑줄 친 <u>that</u>이 이끄는 절에서 주어를 찾아 밑줄을 그으시오.

149 It is necessary to manifest gratitude to the thousands of doctors and researchers all over the world <u>who</u> with great generosity and professionalism dedicate themselves daily with all their strength to the service of the suffering and to the curing of illnesses.

QUESTION 위 문장의 밑줄 친 <u>who</u>가 이끄는 절에서 동사를 찾아 밑줄을 그으시오.

❋ **Advanced Points** 〈접속사 that＋**부사구[절]**＋주어＋동사 ∼〉 또는 〈주격 관계대명사＋**부사구[절]**＋동사 ∼〉의 구조에서는 뒤의 주어나 동사를 놓치기 쉽다. 부사구[절]의 범위를 파악하여 that절의 주어나 관계사절의 동사를 잘 판단하도록 한다.

150 Those who love the world learn with great effort the art of obtaining and enjoying what they love.

151 One way to help keep life's slings and arrows from knocking you off course is to ensure your life is _____, and that way, a setback in any one area won't mean in your mind that you're a complete failure. －모의응용

*slings and arrows ((비유)) 역경, 가혹한 상황

FILL-IN ① straightforward　　② multidimensional

152 Health was for many East Asians both previously and today dependent on the balance of forces in the body and the relationships between every part of the body and almost every other part.

153 Just as inside a living body, the heart, lungs, and bloodstream work constantly to supply <u>oxygen</u> to <u>every living cell</u>, the communication system in an organization supplies its smallest units — the employees — with the most valuable thing: information.

QUESTION 위 문장에서 밑줄 친 oxygen과 every living cell에 대응하는 단어를 찾아 쓰시오.

154 The advocates of the free market economy argue that to be left to itself, unhindered by state intervention, the market will deliver the maximum good to society.

SUMMARY Proponents of the free market claim the freer the economy is, the | greater / lesser | yields the market will get.

155 In fact, there is so much salt in the seas of the world that if it were possible to remove the salt and spread it over, for example, the United States, some people believe it would form a layer a mile thick!

156 When making decisions, make sure to identify your preferences early on; <u>otherwise</u> you may feel overwhelmed by choices that in many ways look identical.

QUESTION 위 문장에서 밑줄 친 otherwise가 의미하는 바로 적절한 것을 고르시오.
① if you don't clarify what you like
② if there are too many choices to handle

157 As wildfire season raged in California this fall, a start-up that with its cutting-edge technology used artificial intelligence to pinpoint the location of blazes there within minutes was in some cases far faster than firefighters would have been.

158 Two languages <u>being</u> at hand, bilingual citizens have many cultural and occupational advantages.

> QUESTION 위 문장에서 밑줄 친 분사의 의미상 주어에 해당되는 것을 찾아 밑줄을 그으시오.

159 A composition in narrative style follows a chronological order, with one action <u>following</u> another, just as things happened in the original experience.

> QUESTION 위 문장에서 밑줄 친 분사의 의미상 주어에 해당되는 것을 찾아 밑줄을 그으시오.

160 With their ability to network and communicate with each other, young people rely on each other's opinions more than marketing messages when <u>making</u> purchase decisions. — 모의

> QUESTION 위 문장에서 밑줄 친 분사의 의미상 주어에 해당되는 것을 찾아 밑줄을 그으시오.

161 <u>Confident</u> about themselves and their abilities, children who have high self-esteem are more likely to fulfill their potential.

> QUESTION 위 문장에서 밑줄 친 분사의 의미상 주어에 해당되는 것을 찾아 밑줄을 그으시오.

Main Points

1. 분사구문의 의미상 주어가 문장의 주어와 다를 때는 분사 앞에 그 의미상 주어를 반드시 써야 한다.
2. 〈with+O+v-ing[p.p.]〉는 문장의 동사와 동시에 일어나는 상황을 나타낸다. O는 분사의 의미상 주어이므로 'O가 v하면서 [v되어]'로 해석한다.
3. 분사구문의 의미를 명확히 하기 위해 분사구문 앞에 접속사를 두기도 한다.
4. being 또는 having been이 생략되어 분사구문이 명사나 형용사로 시작될 수 있다.

162 Our adventures in space have been a hymn of national purpose for a half-century, the many high notes of success colored with gloomy tones of failure.

*hymn 찬가, 찬송가

Advanced Points 의미상 주어를 분사 앞에 써야 하는 경우, 의미상 주어의 형태나 길이, 또는 분사구문의 형태(being이나 having been의 생략) 때문에 〈의미상 주어+분사구문〉의 구조로 판단하기 어려운 경우가 있으므로 주의해야 한다.

163 Of all the thinkers of antiquity, Aristotle was perhaps one of the most comprehensive, his works ranging over the landscape of knowledge, such as physics, politics, and ethics. ㅡ사관학교응용

164 People who cannot accept courtesy when it comes their way feel uneasy if kindness seems to come to them with no strings attached.

165 Machines may sometimes be troublesome, frustrating, and even harmful; once accustomed to the advantages they provide, however, you feel that they are almost indispensable to your daily life. ㅡ경찰대

QUESTION▶ 위 문장의 밑줄 친 분사 accustomed의 의미상 주어에 해당하는 것에 밑줄 그으시오.

166 Distance learning can be particularly helpful if you are trying to pursue a degree while continuing / continued to work full-time.

QUESTION▶ 위 문장의 네모 안에서 어법에 맞는 것을 고르시오.

167 A great questioner, Socrates was a natural philosopher, and many consider him the first moralist in that he urged people to question their own values and the very purpose of living by raising the concept of morality and a code of ethics.

168 Curious about the world around them, children will often find their parents a leading model in their lives for answers.

169 Organizing your life by balancing your responsibilities to the best of your ability is an ongoing project, every step that is achieved increasing your confidence and determination to keep going.

SUMMARY▶ Balancing your tasks will build / lose the momentum you need to persevere.

GOLDEN SAYING

No doubt the truth is hard to
come by for those who do not
like the sound of it — dreams and
illusions are so much more pleasant.

-Anatoli Granovsky ((스웨덴 저술가))

분명히 진실은 그것이 내는 소리를 좋아하지 않는 사람들에게는
얻기 어렵다. 꿈과 환상이 훨씬 더 즐겁다.

생략이 일어난 문장 구조 이해하기

Chapter Overview

문장에 마땅히 있어야 할 것이 없으면 이해하기가 어렵다. 생략이 주로 일어나는 곳과 생략이 일어나는 이유를 알아두는 것이 중요하다.

Chapter Goals

1 반복되어 생략이 일어난 곳과 생략된 어구를 알 수 있다.

2 접속사나 관계사가 생략된 곳을 알 수 있다.

3 if 또는 if절이 생략된 것이 아닌지 살펴봐야 할 문장을 파악할 수 있다.

Must-know
Words &
Lexical
Phrases

U N I T **1 7** •

172 commit (죄 등을) 저지르다

    loyal 충실한, 충성스러운

    presume 가정하다, 추정하다

    cf. **presumed** (당연한 것으로) 여겨지는

173 considering that ~이라는 점에서 보면

    concrete 구체적인

    essential 본질[근본]적인 (=fundamental); 필수적인

    cf. **essence** 본질, 기초; 추출물

174 straightforward 직접적인; 솔직한; 간단한

175 immigrant (다른 나라로 온) 이민(자); 이주민

    (↔emigrant (다른 나라로 가는) 이민자[이주민])

    cf. **immigrate** 이민을 오다 (↔emigrate 이민을 가다)

    (!) **migrant** 이주자; 이주하는

      migrate 이주[이동]하다

176 adversely 부정적으로; 불리하게; 반대로

    bizarre 이상한, 기이한 (=weird, eccentric)

    severely 심하게

178 imitate 모방하다, 따라 하다 (=mimic)

    incorporate (일부로) 포함하다; (법인체를) 설립하다

    initiative 솔선, 선도; 계획

    cf. **take the initiative** 솔선해서[앞장서서] 하다

    (!) **take advantage of** ~을 이용하다

179 statement 진술, 서술, 성명

180 exceptionally 특별히, 유난히; 예외적으로

    cf. **exceptional** 특출한, 우수한; 예외적인

    adapt 각색하다; 적응하다(=adjust); 맞추다, 조정하다

    assess 평가하다(=estimate, evaluate); 재다, 가늠하다

    quote 인용하다; (예를) 들다; 견적을 내다

    cf. **quotation** 인용(구); 견적, 시세

U N I T **1 8** •

181 utility 유용성 (=usefulness)

182 take A into account A를 고려하다

184 alternative 대안(적인); 대체 가능한

   cf. alternative therapy 대체 요법

      alternate (두 가지가) 번갈아 나오는; 하나 거르는;

      번갈아 나오다[나오게 하다]

   validity 효력, 유효(성); 타당성

   cf. valid 유효한; 타당한, 근거 있는 (↔invalid 근거 없는; 무효한)

      validate 입증하다; (법적으로) 유효하게 하다

      validation 입증, 확인

185 facilitate 용이하게 하다; 촉진하다

   controversy 논란; 말다툼

   cf. controversial 논란이 많은

186 define 밝히다; 정의를 내리다

187 intensity 강도, 세기; 강렬함

   cf. intense 극심한, 강렬한; 치열한

   existence 존재, 실재, 현존; 생활, 생계

   distinct 별개의, 구별되는; 뚜렷한, 분명한

188 idolize 우상화하다, 숭배하다

   cf. idol 우상, 숭배물

189 mighty 힘센, 강력한; 거대한; 대단한

   tyrant 폭군, 독재자

   cf. tyranny 독재; 압제, 폭압

UNIT 19 •

191 proponent 지지자 (↔opponent 반대자; (논쟁) 상대)

   inhumane 비인간적인, 잔혹한

   toil 힘들게 일하다; (힘겹게) 움직이다, 나아가다

193 assume 가정하다; (임무 등을) 맡다; (성질을) 띠다

   conviction 확신, 신념; 유죄 판결

   cf. convince 납득시키다, 설득하다 (=persuade)

      convict ((주로 수동태)) 유죄를 선고하다

   differentiate A from B A를 B와 구별하다

194 ensure 보장하다, 반드시 ~하게 하다

195 canal 운하, 수로; (체내의) 관

   formation ((지질)) 층, 지층; 형성(물)

196 around the corner 코앞에 있는, 아주 가까운

197 identity 정체성, 신원; 일치

198 prime 주요한, 주된; 최고의, 뛰어난

199 exhausted 고갈된; 기진맥진한

   cf. exhaust 다 써버리다; 기진맥진하게 만들다; 배기가스

200 individualize 개별화하다; 개성을 뚜렷하게 하다

   achievable 성취할 수 있는

   cf. achieve 성취해 주다

   confirm 확인해 주다; 확정 짓다

   access 이용하다; 접근하다

UNIT 20 •

201 defense 방어물, 방어 수단; 방어

202 delighted 아주 기뻐하는; 즐거워하는

   evolution 진화; 발달

   cf. evolve 진화하다; 발달하다

203 get by 그럭저럭 살아가다; 지나가다, 통과하다

204 chronically 고질적으로; 만성적으로

   cf. chronic 장기간에 걸친, 만성적인 (↔acute 급성의; 격렬한;

     예리[예민]한)

   leak (액체, 기체가) 새다; 새는 곳[구멍]; 누출

   vessel 배, 선박; 그릇; 혈관

   productive 생산적인

   patch 때우다, 덧대다; (헝겊) 조각; 부분

207 incentive 장려책, 보상물; 격려하는, 보상의

   inevitable 불가피한, 필연적인 (=unavoidable)

   regulation 규제, 단속; 규정

   enforce (법을) 시행하다; 강요하다

208 abstract 요약하다; 추출하다; 추상적인; 개요, 발췌

   discipline (지식) 분야, 학과목; 규율, 훈육; 훈육하다; 징계하다

   manuscript (책, 악보 등의) 원고

209 flavor 맛, 풍미; 맛을 내다

   prediction 예측, 예상

UNIT 17 생략·공통구문

170 Opinion is not fact, although if said often enough and loud enough, some people seem to believe it is.

QUESTION 위 문장에서 생략이 일어난 곳을 모두 찾아 ✔로 표시하고 생략된 어구를 쓰시오.

🌱 **Basic Points** 반복되는 어구는 언어의 경제성을 위해서 생략할 수 있다. 따라서 문장에서 어떤 필수 요소가 없다면, 앞에 나온 어구가 반복되어 생략된 것이 아닌지 살펴보자.
1. 등위접속사 뒤, 콤마(,) 자리에 생략어구가 있을 수 있다.
2. be동사나 조동사 뒤, to-v구의 to 또는 to 뒤를 생략하는 경우가 많다.
3. 부사절과 주절의 주어가 같은 경우 부사절에서 〈주어+be동사〉를 생략할 수 있다.
4. 아래와 같은 생략 표현들은 굳이 생략된 어구를 찾지 말고 의미를 숙어처럼 외워두는 것이 좋다.
   - if not: (앞에 나온 어구, 절을 받아) 만약 (〜이) 아니라면
   - if any: 만약 (조금이라도) 있다면
   - if ever: 만약 〜한다고 해도
   - if possible: 가능하다면
   - if necessary: 필요하다면
   - whenever possible: 가능할 때마다 (= whenever it is possible)
   - what if ~?: 〜라면 어떨까?; 〜하더라도 무슨 상관인가?

171 From birth, you absorb and are shaped by the language, values, and patterns of behavior that characterize your own small immediate group.

QUESTION 위 문장에서 밑줄 친 부분에 공통으로 연결되는 어구에 밑줄을 그으시오.

🌱 **Basic Points** 반복되는 요소를 생략하여 두 개 이상의 어구(A, B)가 아래처럼 한 어구(X)에 공통으로 연결되는 경우가 있는데 이를 공통구문이라고 한다. A와 B는 병렬구조를 이룬다.

AX+BX ⇒ (A+B)X   XA+XB ⇒ X(A+B)

172 The most terrible acts committed by humans have often been the ones not of criminals or madmen but of ordinary, loyal citizens acting in the presumed interests of their group against another group.

173 Considering that language is often used simply to describe concrete events in literature, there is no essential difference between literature and film as literature uses words for description and film, pictures.

174 While testing seems the most straightforward evidence about the effectiveness of teaching in schools, it is not necessarily thought to be by the majority of students.

175 For immigrants, contacts with the country of origin are now more frequent, and result in more immigrant families being influenced to maintain cultural patterns from the homeland, and attempt to influence their children to keep them. -모의응용

176 Highly social animals, such as certain types of parrot, seem to be adversely / verbally affected when kept alone. Some parrots will engage in bizarre behaviors and can severely harm themselves. -모의

QUESTION▶ 위 문장의 네모 안에서 문맥에 맞는 낱말로 적절한 것을 고르시오.

177 Failure can be an opportunity if you are willing to change. If not, be prepared to fail again and again as the world attempts to teach you its lessons.

178 The first and best way for a baby to learn that exercise is a lifetime routine is by imitating his or her parents, so you should be your child's role model, incorporating physical activity into your daily routine and involving your child in your workout routine whenever possible. -모의응용

SUMMARY▶ Parents should take the initiative for / advantage of children to form exercise habits.

179 What if your value and the essence of being loved aren't based on how you look or how well you do something? Actually, this concept is not in question, as it is a statement of fact and is entirely true.

180 *Hamlet* became and has remained famous, not only because it is an exceptionally rich and fascinating text, but also because it has been and still is being played, adapted, assessed and quoted.

181 A horse is useless if no one can ride it, a sword if no one can strike with it, and meat if no one can eat it; thus every material utility depends on a related human ability.

QUESTION 위 문장에서 생략이 일어난 곳을 <u>모두</u> 찾아 ✔로 표시하고 생략된 어구를 쓰시오.

🍃 **Main Points** 문장에서 어구가 반복될 때 <u>반복어구는 종종 생략된다.</u> 반복된 어구가 생략되어 의미 이해에 지장이 없더라도 문장 구조상 필요한 것이 없으면 영어 학습자들은 이해하기 어려울 수 있다. 이때는 문맥을 잘 살펴서, 어색한 부분에 앞에 나온 어구를 대입해보는 것이 좋다. 특히 아래와 같은 (A+B+C)(A′+C′) 구조가 자주 등장하므로 잘 알아두자.

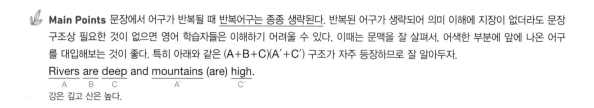
Rivers are deep and mountains (are) high.
　　A　B　C　　　　　A′　　C′
강은 깊고 산은 높다.

182 Students criticized the textbooks for not having interesting activities, and teachers for not taking into account the student's knowledge levels. That's why they did not enjoy using the textbooks.

QUESTION 위 문장에서 생략이 일어난 곳을 찾아 ✔로 표시하고 생략된 어구를 쓰시오.

✳ **Error Points** 문장 구조에만 의지하여 생략된 위치를 판단하면 자칫 오역을 하게 될 수 있다. 위의 예문에서 구조상으로는 and teachers (criticized the textbooks) for not taking ~ 또는 and (students criticized) teachers for not taking ~ 이 두 가지 생략이 모두 가능하기 때문이다. 생략된 반복어구를 정확히 찾으려면 <u>반드시 문맥을 함께 고려해야 한다.</u>

183 Age appears to be best in four things: old wood best to burn, old wine to drink, old friends to trust, and old authors to read. ─Francis Bacon ((英 철학자))

184 Like many other alternative therapies, the popularity of hypnotherapy continues to grow, but there is still debate on the scientific basis of hypnosis, and there is much more on the validity of hypnotherapy.

*hypnotherapy 최면 요법 **hypnosis 최면

185 In a research team, one member might be particularly good at experimental design, another at data analysis, and a third at writing reports; by learning who is good at what, the group facilitates _____.

FILL-IN ① controversy　　② collaboration

186 Most data about social problems can't solve the problems because the data is mostly about how the problem is happening but not about why; to define "why" from the data is the job researchers and policy makers need to focus on.

187 The finding that the intensity of a taste is decreased after trying the same taste, but not after trying a different taste, serves as evidence for the existence of distinct receptors for different tastes. —모의응용   *receptor ((생물)) 감각 기관

188 My political ideal is democracy. Everyone should be respected as an individual, but no one idolized. —Albert Einstein

189 When a person obeys another person merely because the mightier of the two has power and threatens violence, the one giving the orders is a tyrant, and the one obeying them his slave.

190 Painting is sometimes thought to be a higher form of art than cartooning, theater higher than movies, and classic novels higher than "blockbuster" novels.

191 An electric car that its proponents hope will replace horse-drawn carriages at tourist attractions was proposed by those who say it's inhumane to have animals toiling.

QUESTION 위 문장에서 접속사나 관계사가 생략된 부분을 찾아 ✔로 표시하고 생략된 것을 쓰시오.

192 Champions aren't made in gyms. Champions are made from something they have deep inside them — a desire, a dream, a vision. –Muhammad Ali ((美 복싱 선수))

QUESTION 위 문장에서 접속사나 관계사가 생략된 부분을 찾아 ✔로 표시하고 생략된 것을 쓰시오.

 Main Points

1. 접속사 that의 생략

that이 이끄는 명사절이 문장에서 동사의 목적어 역할을 할 때, that은 생략될 수 있다.

S+V+(접속사)+S′+V′ ~
　　　　　　○

2. 관계사의 생략

목적격 관계대명사 who(m), which, that과 관계부사 when, where, why도 종종 생략되며, the way가 선행사일 때 관계부사 how는 함께 쓰일 수 없어 생략되고 how 대신 that 또는 in which를 쓰기도 한다. 따라서 아래와 같은 구조는 명사와 명사 사이에 관계사가 생략된 것이므로, 명사(선행사)와 (대)명사 사이에 적절한 관계사를 보충하여 문장 구조를 파악한다.

　　명사　　+ (관계사)+명사(S′)+V′ ~
　(선행사)↑　　　　　　　　│

193 It may not be valid to assume the media make our time distinct from the past, because we know relatively little about how information was shared in the past. –수능

TOPIC the [conviction / doubt] about whether the media differentiates the present from the past

194 The most important single responsibility of the leader is to ensure harmony and happiness among the people he or she is responsible for.

195 An English engineer and canal builder, William Smith, discovered that each rock formation in the canals he worked on contained fossils unlike those in the beds either above or below. It helped make evident the significance of fossils as geologic tools.

*bed ((지질)) 지층; (강, 바다 등의) 바닥

196 When you want to quit while your destination is just around the corner, it is the time you need to remind yourself that you are just some steps away to your goal and quitting is not an option.

197 High school should be the place young minds begin to develop their own way of looking at the world. It should be a place friendships are made and identities are created.

198 One prime reason international tourism in Europe has developed so strongly since 1945 has been the almost total absence of major political and military conflict in the region since the end of the Second World War.

199 If you saw the way some people treat the world, you would think there is somewhere else to go once the earth's resources have been exhausted. —모의

QUESTION▶ 위 문장이 뜻하는 바로 가장 적절한 것을 고르시오.
① 지구를 대체할 행성을 찾아야 한다. ② 지구 자원을 낭비하지 말아야 한다.

200 Individualized achievable challenge connects students to knowledge by communicating high expectations, confirming that they have the capacity to reach these goals, and showing them how to access the tools and support they need to reach goals they consider desirable. —모의

Plus⁺ 관계부사의 선행사 생략

선행사가 일반적인 시간, 장소, 이유를 나타내는 the time, the place, the reason 등인 경우에는 관계부사 대신 선행사가 흔히 생략된다.
Monday is **(the day)** [when people are most likely to feel blue]. 월요일은 사람들이 우울하다고 느끼기 가장 쉬운 날이다.
It's risky to climb on a branch, but that's **(the place)** [where all the fruit is].
나뭇가지에 올라가는 것은 위험하지만, 그곳이 모든 열매가 있는 장소이다.
This is **(the reason)** [why I've raised the question again]. 이것이 내가 그 질문을 다시 제기한 이유이다.

201 Were it not for the special defenses they have against their enemies, many animals could not survive.

QUESTION 위 문장에서 if가 생략된 절을 찾아 밑줄을 긋고, if를 포함하는 절로 고쳐 쓰시오.

202 Some experts say that were Charles Darwin alive today, he would be delighted with the scientific validation of his theory of evolution.

QUESTION 위 문장에서 if가 생략된 절을 찾아 밑줄을 긋고, if를 포함하는 절로 고쳐 쓰시오.

> **Main Points** if 가정법 문장에서 if가 생략되면 주어와 (조)동사(were, had, should 등)가 도치되어 마치 의문문과 같은 어순이 된다. 이러한 조건절의 형태는 콤마(,) 없이 문장 중간이나 주절 뒤에 오기도 하므로 특히 주의해야 한다.
> If I had known that you were ill, I would have gone to see you.
> → **Had I known** that you were ill, I **would have gone** to see you.
> → I **would have gone** to see you **had I known** that you were ill.
> 네가 아팠던 것을 내가 알았다면, 나는 너를 보러 갔을 텐데.
> 접속사나 관계사가 없는데 두 개의 절이 결합되어 있고 과거형 조동사가 있으면 if가 생략된 가정법이 아닌지 살펴본다.

203 When we pack, we are sometimes amazed to find that we don't need very many things to live. We wouldn't normally believe we could get by with such a tiny amount of stuff.

QUESTION 위 두 번째 문장에서 생략된 if절을 고르시오.
① if we never packed
② if we were amazed

> **Advanced Points** if절 전체가 문장에서 생략되는 경우도 있다. 문장에 과거형 조동사가 포함되어 있으면 가정의 의미가 함축되어 있는 것은 아닌지 판단해야 한다.

204 Should you find yourself in a chronically leaking boat, energy devoted to changing vessels is likely to be more productive than energy devoted to patching leaks. –Warren Buffett ((美 투자가))

205 The piano could hardly have become so popular, had the music written for it not occupied a position at the top of European culture.

QUESTION 위 문장의 내용과 일치하는 것을 고르시오.
① 피아노를 위해 쓰인 음악 덕분에 피아노가 인기를 끌었다.
② 실제로 피아노가 유럽 문화에서 대중화된 것은 아니었다.

206 People who lack the inner skill of confidence don't try to accomplish what they might have the ability to accomplish were they confident and did try.

207 Rules and incentives are an inevitable and necessary part of our social and political life — the banking crisis would have been far less serious had Depression era regulations not been removed and had existing regulations been enforced. ─사관학교

208 Indeed, abstracting is difficult for people in every discipline. Many famous novelists have written to their editors that they regretted the extreme length of their manuscripts; had they had more time, the work would have been half / twice as long.

QUESTION▶ 위 문장의 네모 안에서 문맥에 맞는 낱말로 적절한 것을 고르시오.

209 Judgments about flavor are often influenced by predictions based on the appearance of the food. For example, red foods would be expected to be strawberry-flavored. ─모의응용

210 The most difficult fact in the world could have been faced when it was simple, and the biggest problem in the world could have been solved when it was small. The simple fact that someone finds no problem big from the beginning is that person's prime achievement.

GOLDEN SAYING

The best equipment a young man
can have for the battle of life is
a conscience, common sense
and good health.

-Ernest Hemingway

인생이라는 전투를 대비하여 젊은이가 가질 수 있는 최고의 장비는
양심, 상식, 그리고 건강이다.

어순에 주의해야 하는 구문

Chapter Overview

문장을 이루는 S, V, O, C는 본래의 자리를 벗어나 이동하는 경우가 있다. 이러한 이동은 문장을 이해하기 어렵게 만들기도 하지만, 나름의 규칙이 있다. 그 규칙을 이해하면 문장 이해가 더 쉬워지고 영어의 묘미를 느낄 수 있을 것이다.

Chapter Goals

1 문법적으로 어순이 변하는 주요 구문을 나열할 수 있다.

2 주어가 아닌 다른 어구를 <u>문장 앞으로</u> 보내는 이유를 말할 수 있다.

3 어구를 <u>문장 뒤로</u> 보내는 이유를 말할 수 있다.

4 이미 언급된 정보인지 새로운 정보인지에 따른 어구의 자연스러운 위치를 말할 수 있다.

Must-know
Words &
Lexical
Phrases

UNIT 2 1 •

211 multiply (수, 양을) 크게 증가[증대]시키다; 곱하다

212 abundant 넘칠 정도로 많은, 풍부한 (=plentiful)

   cf. **abundance** 풍부; 부유함

215 cyclical 순환하는, 주기적인 (=cyclic)

   reassure 안심시키다

   cf. **reassure A that** A에게 ~라고 안심시키다

   endure 견디다, 참다(=tolerate); 오래가다[지속되다]

   constant 지속적인, 끊임없는 (=continuous); 변함없는 (=invariable)

216 peculiar 특이한, 독특한 (=unusual); 이상한 (=odd)

   correlation 상관관계, 연관성

   at times 때때로

217 reliability 신뢰성

   cf. **reliable** 믿을 수 있는 (=dependable, trustworthy)

219 hatred 증오(감), 혐오(감)

   noble 고귀한; 귀족의

   absurd 터무니없는, 우스꽝스러운 (=ridiculous)

UNIT 2 2 •

222 endeavor 노력(하다), 시도(하다)

   cf. **endeavor to-v** v하려고 노력하다

223 existence 생활; 존재

224 confront 직면하다, 맞서다; (문제가) 닥치다

   cf. **be confronted with** ~에 직면하다 (=face up to)

   conceptually 개념적으로

   hypothesis ((복수형 hypotheses)) 가설; 추측

225 in the sense ~라는 점에서

   ever- '언제나, 늘, 항상'의 의미의 접두사

   cf. **ever-present** 항상 존재하는

   widen 넓어지다

   complexity 복잡함, 복잡성

   external 외부의 (↔internal 내부의)

226 **seemingly** 겉보기에는, 외견상으로

227 **vanish** 사라지다, 없어지다 (=disappear)

   barrier 장벽, 장애물

228 **composition** 구성, 구성 요소들; 작품; 작곡

   cf. **compose** 구성하다; 작곡하다

      composer 작곡가

   nanoscale 나노 규모의, 아주 작은

231 **imprudent** 경솔한, 현명하지 못한

232 **integrity** 진실성; 완전한 상태, 온전함

   cf. **integral** 완전한; 필수적인

   corruption 부패, 타락; 오염, 변질

   cf. **corrupt** 부패한, 타락한; 오염된; 타락시키다; 오염시키다

   immune system 면역 체계

U N I T 2 3 •

234 **substance** 물질; 핵심, 요지; 실체

   cf. **substantial** (양, 중요성이) 상당한; 크고 튼튼한

   pollen 꽃가루, 화분(花粉)

236 **fanciful** 공상[상상]의, 비현실적인

237 **withhold** 주지 않다, 보류하다; 억제하다

238 **medieval** 중세의, 중세시대의

   pave (도로를) 포장하다

   occasionally 가끔

   cf. **occasional** 가끔의

239 **multitude** 일반 대중 (=crowd); 다수

   privilege 특권(을 주다), 특혜(를 주다)

   cf. **privileged** 특권을 가진

240 **metaphor** 비유, 은유

   accessible 볼 수 있는; 접근[이용]하기 쉬운

241 **persist** (집요하게) 지속하다, 계속하다

243 **distinctive** 독특한; 뚜렷이 구별되는

   in that ~라는 점에서

   reserve 남겨두다; (권한 등을) 갖다, 보유하다; 예약하다

   notable 유명 인사, 중요 인물; 주목할 만한; 유명한

U N I T 2 4 •

245 **wilderness** 황무지, 황야

   shiver (추위 등으로) 떨다; 전율; ((복수형)) 오한, 몸서리

   be worth A[v-ing] A의[v할] 가치가 있다

   majestic 장엄한, 웅장한

246 **accumulate** 축적하다; 쌓이다

   overlie(-overlay-overlain) (지층이) 위에 겹치다; ~의 위에 가로놓이다

   cf. **overlying** 겹친, 위에 가로놓인

   molecular ((화학)) 분자

   exhaustion 고갈, 소진

   cf. **exhaust** 고갈시키다, 다 써버리다

247 **in the nick of time** 때마침, 아슬아슬하게 때를 맞추어

248 **fragile** 연약한, 깨지기 쉬운 (=frail); 섬세한

   irreplaceable 대체[대신]할 수 없는 (=priceless)

   (↔replaceable 대신할 수 있는)

   cf. **replace** 대신하다, 대체하다

   repository (지식 따위의) 보고(寶庫); 저장소

   extinguish 소멸시키다; (불을) 끄다; 끝내다

   constitute 구성하다; 제정하다; 임명하다

   diminish 감소하다; (명성 등을) 손상시키다, 약화시키다[되다]

249 **cope with** ~에 대처하다

   myriad 무수한; 무수함, 무수히 많음

   collapse 폭락(하다); 붕괴(하다)

   fertility 출생률; (토지의) 비옥함; 풍부, 풍요

   cf. **fertile** 생식능력 있는; (토지가) 비옥한; 풍부한

   migration 이동, 이주

   top 능가하다; 위에 얹다

   account for ~의 원인이 되다; 설명하다

   emission 배출(물)

   cf. **emit** 배출하다, 내뿜다

251 **in time** 결국; 시간에 늦지 않게

252 **retain** 유지하다, 보유하다

UNIT 21 어순 변화

211 An error does not become truth by reason of multiplied propagation, <u>nor does truth become error</u> because nobody sees it. –Mahatma Gandhi

*propagation (사상 등의) 선전, 전파

QUESTION 위 문장에서 밑줄 친 절의 주어를 찾아 쓰시오.

> **Basic Points** 영어 문장을 이루는 단어들이 항상 기본 어순을 지켜서 나오는 것은 아니다. 위치가 변하는 데에는 여러 이유가 있는데, 우선 문법적으로 도치가 일어나거나 어순이 변화하는 주요 구문부터 정리해보자.
> 1. 〈so[neither, nor]+V[조동사]+S〉
> 2. 〈There+V+S〉
> 3. 〈명사/형용사/부사+as+S′+V′〉: 비록 S′가 V′하지만[하더라도] (as가 이끄는 양보절의 도치)
> 4. if가 생략된 가정법 (≪ Unit 20)

212 After non-stop rehearsals and diligent planning, when the campus-wide festival came around, enthusiasm was abundant and so was creativity.

213 Food eaten without desire is difficult for the body to absorb nutrients from, and so is / are study done without interest difficult for the mind to process effectively.

QUESTION 위 문장의 네모 안에서 어법상 적절한 것을 고르시오.

214 We had career lessons and were instructed on how to find the right career path, but I had no idea what I wanted to do with my life, and neither did the majority of my classmates.

215 Understanding the cyclical nature of life will reassure you that difficult times won't last forever, and you will feel joy and happiness again. The rough times must be endured and taken as they come, but they are not constant, nor do they last forever. –모의

216 There exists a peculiar correlation between what is in front of our eyes and what is in our heads: large thoughts at times requiring large views, <u>new thoughts new places.</u> —수능응용

QUESTION▶ 위 문장에서 밑줄 친 부분에 생략된 것을 찾아 쓰시오.

217 There are websites containing the answers to nearly any question about which you might be curious. Still, you must be careful to check the reliability of your source.

218 Although there are international agreements signed by some governments, people are killing whales without considering what impact this will have in the future. —모의응용

219 <u>Interested as I am in the physical universe</u>, it is in man, in his loves and hatreds, his noble achievements and absurd failures, that I am more interested. —Albert Einstein

QUESTION▶ 위 문장의 밑줄 친 부분과 의미가 같은 것을 고르시오.
① Because I am interested in the physical universe
② Though I am interested in the physical universe

220 Much as we resemble one another, we are none of us exactly alike, and I have seen no reason why I should not, so far as I could, choose my own course.

221 Not until a geologist closely examines the fossils in the layers for the presence or absence of certain organisms can he or she recognize the gap in time.

QUESTION ▶ 위 문장에서 주절의 주어를 찾아 밑줄을 그으시오.

✎ **Main Points** 부정어구(not, no, never, little, hardly, scarcely, rarely, only 등)를 강조하기 위해 문장 맨 앞에 놓게 되면, 주어-(조)동사의 위치가 〈(조)동사+주어〉 어순으로 서로 뒤바뀌는 도치가 반드시 일어난다.
부사구나 보어를 강조하기 위해 문장 맨 앞에 놓을 때도 동사-주어의 순서로 도치가 일어날 수 있다.

222 Being a human, not always have I done the right thing, nor am I completely proud of every decision I have made, but I've learned from my mistakes and endeavor to improve.

223 Some people say the best way to be happy in life is to have a lot of money, but rarely does money appear to open the way for a more meaningful, exciting existence.

224 Only when confronted with solid experimental evidence or conceptually simpler hypotheses forcing them to new perspectives do scientists change their scientific theories. ─모의응용

QUESTION ▶ 위 문장의 주어를 찾아 밑줄을 그으시오.

225 Not only are humans unique in the sense that they began to use an ever-widening tool set, but we are also the only species on this planet that has constructed forms of complexity that use external energy sources. ─모의

226 Behind a seemingly effortless performance of professional music and theater are years of hard work and training.

QUESTION ▶ 위 문장의 주어를 찾아 밑줄을 그으시오.

227 Science and art belong to the whole world, and before them vanish the barriers of nationality. — Johann Wolfgang von Goethe ((괴테, 독일 작가))

228 Now available to scientists are technologies and equipment to measure the composition and structure of matter on a nanoscale.

229 More obvious is the fact that people who spend their lives watching television do not read as much as they ought to.

230 Hidden in our minds are our belief systems, which have been built from the moment we came into the world by our parents, family, culture, environment, and our education and ultimately shape our own attitudes and behaviors.

231 So imprudent are we that we waste our lives thinking about the future, a time in which we are influential / powerless, rather than focusing on the present, the time in which we have control. — 수능응용

QUESTION 위 문장의 네모 안에서 문맥에 맞는 낱말로 적절한 것을 고르시오.

232 Integrity is the key to defending ourselves against the virus of corruption, like an element in one's immune system; such a crucial one is its role that not only individuals, but systems and institutions too need it.

233 The computer has made possible vast gains in industrial productivity and global communication.

> QUESTION 위 문장에서 목적어를 이루는 어구에 밑줄을 그으시오.

234 The reason is not known why allergy to particular substances, such as pollen, metal, or food, occurs in some people and not in others.

> QUESTION 위 문장에서 주어를 수식하는 어구에 밑줄을 그으시오.

🌱 **Main Points** 영어는 상대적으로 길이가 길거나 문법적으로 복잡한 요소를 가급적 문장 뒤에 두는 특성이 있다. 이 원칙이 적용되는 대표적인 예는 다음과 같다.

1. 가주어/가목적어 it의 사용 (◁ Unit 41)

2. 긴 목적어: 목적어가 수식어구 등이 붙어 길어지고 뒤에 나오는 목적격보어나 부사구는 상대적으로 짧은 경우가 있다. 이를 본래 어순인 SVOC 또는 SVOM으로 표현하면 각각의 범위가 불분명해져 문장을 이해하기 어려워진다. 이를 해결하기 위해 O와 C/M의 순서를 바꾸어 긴 목적어를 문장 뒤로 보낸다.

   SVO~~~C → SVCO~~~
   SVO~~~M → SVMO~~~

3. 주어와 관계사절[형용사구]/주어와 동격어구: 〈주어＋관계사절[형용사구]〉이나 〈주어＋동격어구〉에서 동사 이후인 술부가 매우 짧으면 문장을 이루는 요소 간에 균형이 맞지 않게 된다. 이 경우, 주어 뒤의 관계사절 등을 술부 뒤로 보내기도 한다.

   S[관계사절/형용사구]V~ → SV~[관계사절/형용사구]
   S[동격어구]V~ → SV~[동격어구]

   In a world of free competition, the man grows rich [who is energetic and astute].
   　　　　　　　　　　　　　　　S　　　　V

   자유 경쟁 세계에서, 활동적이고 민첩한 사람이 부유해진다.

235 By inviting parents to participate in childhood education programs, teachers have left open the possibility of collaborating with children and adults and expanding the community.

236 Astronomers no longer regard as fanciful the idea that they may one day pick up signals which have been sent by intelligent beings on other worlds.

237 Experts in education recommend that teachers withhold their personal opinions in classroom discussions as the position of the teacher carries with it an authority that might influence some students to accept the teacher's opinion without question and thus miss the point of the activity. −모의응용

238 The streets of medieval cities were sadly far below ideal; they were not always paved, though occasionally one finds in medieval records a note of the payment for a street to be covered in stone.

239 Science has brought within the reach of the multitudes benefits and advantages that were only available to privileged people up until recently.

TOPIC the [positive role / social problem] of science

240 In Plato's famous cave metaphor, prisoners were imagined tied in such a way that they saw only the shadows of passers-by and they believed the shadows to be real — never guessing the complex reality that was accessible if they would but turn their heads.

241 Although competition has contributed a lot to the development of society, it remains true that conditions continue to persist that make it hard for us to stay calm and be free of anxiety.

242 Because of some research showing that people already get plenty of vitamins from the food they eat, the question is often asked whether multivitamins should be taken each day.

QUESTION 위 문장에서 밑줄 친 the question의 구체적인 내용을 고르시오.
① 종합비타민을 매일 먹어야 하는지 ② 음식으로 충분한 비타민을 섭취할 수 있는지

243 Wagner's *The Ring of the Nibelungs* is distinctive in that it is almost entirely operatic; also unusual is the fact that the libretti for his operas were written by the composer himself — a task normally reserved for a poet or literary notable. -경찰대

*libretto ((복수형 libretti)) 오페라의 대본

244 Greek vases were decorated with detailed paintings showing daily life, hunts, gods, and festivals. Much of what we know about ancient Greek life we learned by studying these vases.

QUESTION ▶ 두 번째 문장에서 주어와 동사를 찾아 S, V로 표시하시오.

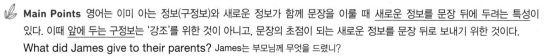

Main Points 영어는 이미 아는 정보(구정보)와 새로운 정보가 함께 문장을 이룰 때 <u>새로운 정보를 문장 뒤에 두려는 특성이</u> 있다. 이때 앞에 두는 구정보는 '강조'를 위한 것이 아니고, 문장의 초점이 되는 새로운 정보를 문장 뒤로 보내기 위한 것이다.

What did James give to their parents? James는 부모님께 무엇을 드렸니?
— He gave them(= their parents) a thank you card. 그는 부모님께 감사 카드를 드렸어.
　　　　　이미 아는 정보　　　　　　　새로운 정보

Who did James give a thank you card to? James는 감사 카드를 누구에게 드렸니?
— He gave a thank you card to their parents. 그는 감사 카드를 부모님께 드렸어.
　　　　　이미 아는 정보　　　　　　　새로운 정보

이미 아는 정보인지는 this, these, it 등의 어구(한정사, 대명사 등)로 표현되고 문맥을 통해서도 알 수 있다.

245 Camping in the wilderness, we spent the first few nights shivering in a shaky tent and guarded against the icy wind. These hardships we endured, and I thought it was worth it because we could see a majestic sunrise the next morning.

246 The accumulated layers of energy-rich organic matter, such as land plants and marine life, were gradually turned into coal and oil by the pressure of the overlying earth. The energy stored in their molecular structure we can now release by burning. —경찰대응용

TOPIC ▶ the ⟨ exhaustion / origin ⟩ of fossil fuels like coal and oil

247 Influencer marketing arrived in the nick of time and has allowed brands to regain the attention of their consumers. Behind this success lies a profitable collaboration between advertisers and influencers.

248 We must consider the status of African-American English as that of an endangered species in need of protection. <u>If we don't</u>, we can expect this fragile, irreplaceable repository where history and community are kept to become extinct, and along with it will be extinguished much of what constitutes their identity. — 경찰대응용

> **QUESTION** 밑줄 친 <u>If we don't</u>가 의미하는 바로 적절한 것을 고르시오.
> ① If we ignore the diminishing of African-American English
> ② If we don't replace African-American English

249 Cities across the globe are coping with myriad challenges, from collapsing fertility, migration from rural areas and the disappearance of the middle class. Topping these is the fact that cities account for a huge amount of greenhouse gas emissions worldwide.

250 Managing risks to stay competitive is a challenge many businesses are facing and linked to this is the importance of having the right talent, the right team and the right capability to make such decisions.

251 So many things my teacher told me I will understand in time and I can't wait to see how the seeds he planted within me grow.

252 With a growth mindset, individuals are more likely to continue working hard, and that, however tough it is to work with, they will retain until they achieve their goals. *growth mindset 성장형 사고방식 ((노력을 통한 더 나은 변화를 믿는 사고방식을 가리키는 심리학 용어))

GOLDEN SAYING

Happy is the man who has broken
the chains which hurt the mind,
and has given up worrying
once and for all.

-Ovid ((고대 로마 시인))

마음을 다치게 하는 사슬을 끊어버리고
걱정하기를 완전히 그만둔 사람은 행복하다.

CHAPTER 07

병렬구조를 파악하기 어려운 이유

Chapter Overview

때로는 가장 쉬워 보이는 것이 문장을 이해하는 것을 어렵게 한다. 긴 문장에서 자주 등장하는 흔한 접속사인 and, but, or가 그중의 하나이다.

이 접속사들이 무엇과 무엇을 연결하는지 정확히 파악하는 것이 중요하다.

Chapter Goals

1 병렬구조를 이루는 접속사를 나열할 수 있다.
2 〈A+접속사+B〉에서 병렬로 연결된 A와 B가 무엇인지 알 수 있다.

UNIT 25 •

254 **variation** 차이, 변화

    extent 정도, 규모

255 **guilt** 죄책감; 유죄 (↔innocence 결백, 무죄)

    resentment 분노, 분개

256 **foster** 기르다, 촉진하다 (=promote); 양육하다

257 **sophisticated** 정교한; 세련된

    reassuring 안심하게 하는

    credibility 신뢰성 (=reliability)

    cf. **credible** 믿을 수 있는 (↔incredible 믿을 수 없는)

    biased 편향된, 편견을 가진 (↔unbiased 편향되지 않은)

    comprehensive 포괄적인, 종합적인

    utterly 전적으로, 완전히 (=totally)

    factual 사실에 입각한

258 **urge** 촉구하다, 재촉하다; 충동; 자극

    have A in common A라는 공통점이 있다

    cf. **have a lot in common** 공통점이 많다

        have little in common 공통점이 거의 없다

259 **medium** 매체; 도구, 수단

    innate 고유의; 선천적인, 타고난

    transaction 교류; 거래; (업무의) 처리

    norm 규범 (=rule); 표준 (=standard)

260 **wealth** 자원, 귀중한 산물; 부, 재산

262 **cue** 단서, 신호

    empathy 공감, 감정이입

UNIT 26 •

263 **intrigue** 흥미를 유발하다; 음모를 꾸미다

264 **surmount** 극복하다; (산을) 오르다

265 **reminder** 상기시키는 것

    prompt 자극물; 신속한; 시간을 엄수하는; 유도하다

266 **flexibility** 융통성, 유연함; 구부리기 쉬움

    inclination (~하려는) 경향, 의향; 경사(도)

    cf. **incline (to)** (~쪽으로) 기울다; 마음이 기울다

    compromise 타협(하다)

단어를 미리 알면, 구문 학습이 더 쉬워져요!

267 **constant** 일정한, 변함없는; 끊임없는

 herbivore 초식동물

 ⓘ **carnivore** 육식동물

 omnivore 잡식동물

268 **be keen to-v** v하려고 열을 올리다, v할 것을 열망하다

 abuse 오용, 남용; 오용[남용]하다

 stand for ~을 지지[옹호]하다; ~을 상징[대표]하다

 (↔stand up to ~에 저항하다[맞서다])

 guarantee 보장하다; 보장; 보증서

269 **substitute A for B** B를 A로 대체하다

 (=substitute[replace] B with A)

270 **reversed** 거꾸로 된, 반대의

271 **mediation** 중재, 조정

 cf. **mediate** (중간에서) 조정[중재]하다, 화해시키다

 parallel 유사하다; 필적하다; 평행(한); 유사(한)

 advocacy 옹호, 지지

 cf. **advocate** 옹호[지지]하다; 옹호[지지]자; 변호인

 in so far as ~하는 한

 negotiation 협상, 협의

 neutral 중립(의)

UNIT **27** •—————————————————

274 **medication** 약(물); 약물치료

 counterproductive 역효과를 낳는

275 **frustration** 좌절감; 불만

 cf. **frustrated** 좌절감을 느끼는; 불만스러운

276 **trivialize** 하찮게 여기다, 사소하게 만들다

 cf. **trivial** 사소한, 하찮은

 mainstream 주류, 대세; 주류에 편입하다

 profound 심오한, 깊은; 엄청난

277 **offender** 범죄자

 eliminate 없애다, 제거하다; 탈락시키다

 inequality 불평등 (↔equality 평등)

279 **influential** 영향력 있는

 capitalism 자본주의

 cf. **capital** 자본(금); (나라의) 수도

 destruction 파괴

 cf. **destruct** 파괴하다 (=destroy)

 perpetual 영구적인; 빈번한; 끊임없는

280 **perceive** 인지하다, 인식하다

282 **disastrous** 형편없는, 처참한

 miscalculation 잘못된 판단, 계산 착오

 check-up (건강) 검진

 commit A to B A(돈, 시간)를 B에 쓰다; A가 B에 전념[헌신]하다

 moderate 적당한, 알맞은; 중간의; 완화하다

UNIT **28** •

283 **controversial** 논란이 많은

284 **insight** 통찰력

288 **deficiency** 부족, 결핍 (=shortage); 결함, 불완전

 cf. **deficient** 부족한; 결함이 있는

 compensate (for) (결점 등을) 보완하다; 보상[배상]하다

 persistent 지속적인; 끈기 있는

 cf. **persist** 계속[지속]하다

289 **rust** (금속이) 녹슬다; 녹

 disuse 사용하지 않음, 폐기

 purity 맑음; 순수성; 순도

 inaction 나태함, 게으름; 활동 부족

 vigor 활력, 활기, 힘

 cf. **vigorous** 활기찬

290 **dismiss** 묵살하다; 해고하다; 해산시키다

 cf. **dismissal** 묵살; 해고; 해산

 rationality 합리성, 이치에 맞음; 추리력

 cf. **rational** 합리적인, 이성적인 (↔irrational 비합리적인, 비이성적인)

291 **come across** 우연히 마주치다[발견하다]; 이해되다

 outwardly 겉으로는

 cf. **outward** 겉보기에; 밖으로 향하는

293 **buy into** ~을 받아들이다, 믿다; ~의 주식을 사들이다

 pocket (주변과는 이질적인 작은) 집단, 지역; 주머니

 simultaneously 동시에, 일제히

 cf. **simultaneous** 동시의, 동시에 일어나는

253 When dealing with a problem, slowing down provides time to consider how the issue has been framed ⬚and⬚ whether we have really considered all the relevant factors. −모의응용

QUESTION 위 문장에서 ⬚and⬚가 연결하고 있는 부분에 밑줄을 그으시오.

Ⅴ **Basic Points** 등위접속사 and, but, or 뒤에서 두 개 이상의 어구(A, B)가 한 어구(X)에 공통으로 연결되는 구조를 병렬구조라 한다.

XA and XB → XA ⬚and⬚ B = X ⎡A
⎢⬚and⬚
⎣B

연결되는 어구(A, B)는 문법적으로 대등한 형태이며, 대표적인 예는 다음과 같다.
- 명사 ⬚and⬚ 명사
- 부사 ⬚and⬚ 부사
- v-ing ⬚and⬚ v-ing
- 전명구 ⬚and⬚ 전명구
- 형용사 ⬚and⬚ 형용사
- 동사 ⬚and⬚ 동사
- to-v ⬚and⬚ (to-)v
- 절 ⬚and⬚ 절

아래와 같은 상관접속사로 연결되는 구조에서도 A와 B가 병렬구조를 이룬다.
- both A ⬚and⬚ B   A와 B 둘 다
- neither A ⬚nor⬚ B   A도 B도 아닌
- not only[just, merely, simply] A ⬚but⬚ (also) B A뿐만 아니라 B도 (= B as well as A)
- either A ⬚or⬚ B   A와 B 둘 중 하나
- not A ⬚but⬚ B   A가 아니라 B (= B but not A)

병렬구조에서는 연결된 어구인 A와 B가 무엇인지를 정확히 파악하는 게 중요하다. and, but, or 뒤의 B의 형태를 보고 앞에서 이와 대등한 어구를 찾아 문맥으로 확인한다.

254 Variations in residents' feelings about tourism's relationship to environmental damage are related to the type of tourism, the extent to which residents feel the natural environment needs to be protected, and the distance residents live from the tourist attractions. −수능

255 Guilt is anger directed at ourselves — at what we did or did not do. Resentment is anger directed at others — at what they did or did not do.

−Peter McWilliams ((美 작가))

256 Creative thinking is fostered in classrooms where children are given opportunities to explore new materials and ideas, and to construct new knowledge and skills.

257 To attract and impress audiences, the news media employ sophisticated techniques that project a reassuring appearance of credibility and that make their stories seem biased / unbiased , comprehensive, and utterly factual.

QUESTION▶ 위 문장의 네모 안에서 문맥에 맞는 낱말로 적절한 것을 고르시오.

258 Critics of group work urge that schools reexamine their policies and allow some students to work on their own. They believe there is no reason to make some students cooperate with other students with whom they have little in common and for whom they do the lion's share of the work.

*the lion's share (몫을 나눈 것 중에서) 가장 큰 몫

259 Language is the medium through which groups preserve their innate cultures, educational transactions take place and norms and laws are established.

260 Without government support of the arts, there would be a great deal of cultural wealth lost because of the lack of power to either promote creation or protect it for future generations. ─모의응용

261 Make progress every day. We understand that life is not always about dramatic change, but more often about the small steps and achievements we make each day.

262 Animals — and people — who have been raised in extreme social isolation are poor at reading emotional cues in those around them not because they lack the basic circuitry for empathy but because, lack / lacking emotional tutors, they have never learned to pay attention to these messages so haven't practiced this skill. ─모의

*circuitry 신경 회로(망); (전기) 회로망

QUESTION▶ 위 문장의 네모 안에서 어법상 적절한 표현을 고르시오.

연결어구의 후보가 두 개 이상인 문장

263 Instead of trying to get children to buckle down, why not focus on getting them to take pleasure in meaningful, productive activity which intrigues them to take steps toward learning new skills and natural joy in learning what they want to learn?

*buckle down 본격적으로 시작하다; 온 힘을 쏟다

QUESTION 위 문장에서 밑줄 친 natural joy와 and로 연결된 부분에 밑줄을 그으시오.

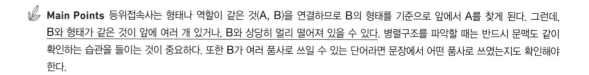 **Main Points** 등위접속사는 형태나 역할이 같은 것(A, B)을 연결하므로 B의 형태를 기준으로 앞에서 A를 찾게 된다. 그런데, B와 형태가 같은 것이 앞에 여러 개 있거나, B와 상당히 멀리 떨어져 있을 수 있다. 병렬구조를 파악할 때는 반드시 문맥도 같이 확인하는 습관을 들이는 것이 중요하다. 또한 B가 여러 품사로 쓰일 수 있는 단어라면 문장에서 어떤 품사로 쓰였는지도 확인해야 한다.

264 Don't think of today as just another day of your life but a grand opportunity nature has offered you to surmount the hurdles you couldn't surmount yesterday.

QUESTION 위 문장에서 밑줄 친 just another day of your life와 but으로 연결된 부분에 밑줄을 그으시오.

265 We recall information that we've learned most effectively when we're given reminder prompts, such as the initial letter of a required word, and when we are presented with a good memory trigger, the relevant "memory web" draws the memory out.

QUESTION 위 문장에서 and로 연결된 부분에 밑줄을 그으시오.

✳ **Advanced Points** 때로는 등위접속사 뒤의 B의 범위가 매우 넓을 수 있다. 또한 등위접속사는 앞 절 전체와 뒷 절 전체를 연결하는 경우도 많다는 것을 염두에 두고 연결되는 대상을 찾는다.

266 The ability to maintain some flexibility in both your ideas and your habits will decrease your inclination to disagree and increase your ability to compromise and move toward a solution.

QUESTION 위 문장에서 and로 연결된 부분에 밑줄을 그으시오.

267 The odor of a flower is usually constant, while color can appear different under different lighting conditions, and shape changes with damage from wind and herbivores.

268 Unless we ensure to the enemies of freedom the liberties which they are keen to abuse, then we deny the essence of what we ultimately stand for and are therefore no better than those to whom we are opposed.

–John Stuart Mill ((英 철학자))

SUMMARY Freedom should always be ⌈limited / guaranteed⌉, even to the people who abuse it.

269 Substitute yogurt, low-fat milk, avocados for heavy cream, or fresh herbs for salt, and you'll lower risks for heart disease, diabetes, and other diseases.

*diabetes 당뇨병

270 We spend a lot of time in teaching children how to read, less in teaching them how to speak, and hardly any in teaching them how to listen, but the importance of these skills in business is <u>essentially reversed</u>. –모의응용

QUESTION 위 문장에서 밑줄 친 <u>essentially reversed</u>가 의미하는 바로 적절한 것을 고르시오.
① There is a lack of communication education in the business field.
② Speaking and listening are more important skills than reading in business.

271 Mediation parallels advocacy in so far as it tends to involve a process of negotiation, ⌈but⌉ <u>differs</u> in so far as mediation involves adopting a neutral role between two opposing parties rather than supporting the case of one party against another. –수능응용

QUESTION 위 문장에서 밑줄 친 <u>differs</u>와 ⌈but⌉으로 연결된 대상에 밑줄을 그으시오.

272 Marketing focuses on the needs of the consumer, ultimately benefiting the seller as well. When a product or service is truly marketed, the needs of the consumer are considered from the very beginning of the new product development process, and the product-service mix is designed to meet the unsatisfied needs of the consuming public. –모의

273 What culture does is take what is available in the physical and human environment, interpret it socially [and] fill it with socially shared meaning and feeling. — 사관학교

QUESTION 위 문장에서 [and]가 연결하고 있는 부분에 밑줄을 그으시오.

🖋 **Main Points** 한 문장에 여러 등위접속사가 포함되어 있으면 각각 연결하는 것이 혼동될 수 있다. 연결어구 A, B는 형태와 역할이 같다는 것을 잊지 말고, 범위가 매우 넓은 경우도 있으므로 문맥도 고려해서 판단해야 한다.

274 There are many medications that are safe and effective when taken alone, [but] ineffective or counterproductive when taken in combination with something else.

QUESTION 위 문장에서 [but]이 연결하고 있는 부분에 밑줄을 그으시오.

275 Time pressure leads to frustration, and when we are frustrated or experience other negative emotions, our thinking becomes narrower and less creative. — 모의

276 If we trivialize art and remove it from the core of a mainstream education, we not only deny our students full access to one of humankind's most profound experiences, but miss countless opportunities to understand the important role art plays in culture. — 모의응용

277 What liberals believe is that the fundamental problem originates in society, not in the offenders themselves, and that the best strategy for preventing violent crime is to eliminate poverty and inequality by creating jobs and providing social services.

278 Although it's not uncommon for women to play sports and for men to become nurses, society still has some pretty clear definitions of what men and women should do, how they should handle situations, and what responsibilities they should take care of.

279 Joseph Schumpeter, an influential economist, expressed the view that the essence of capitalism is the process of "creative destruction" — the perpetual cycle of destroying the old and less efficient product or service and replacing it with new, more efficient ones. −사관학교

280 Everyone has stress in their lives. Sometimes emotional reactions to perceived or actual challenges, demands, threats or changes are helpful, and give you the rush of adrenaline you need to get somewhere on time or motivate yourself to get things done.

281 When your attention is not on the present moment but on something else, you will tend to compare even good experiences with others, or you will wonder about future experiences instead of enjoying the present one, and regret / regretting past experiences because they are already over. −수능응용

QUESTION▶ 위 문장의 네모 안에서 어법과 문맥상 적절한 것을 고르시오.

282 Overly positive assumptions can lead to disastrous miscalculations — make us less likely to get health check-ups or wear a cycle helmet, and more likely to commit all of our money to a bad investment — but mild optimism protects and inspires us: it keeps us moving forward rather than backward.

SUMMARY▶ Keeping optimism moderate / high creates positive outcomes.

등위접속사 뒤의 삽입어구에 주의하라

283 It became more common for artists to determine individually the appearance and content of their own work, and, in their search for new forms of self-expression, to make art that was often very controversial. –사관학교응용

QUESTION 위 문장에서 and가 연결하고 있는 부분에 밑줄을 그으시오.

✒ **Main Points** 〈A+등위접속사+**수식어구[삽입어구]**+B〉의 구조로 등위접속사 뒤에 앞뒤로 콤마(,)를 둔 어구가 있으면 일단 삽입된 어구[절]로 봐야 한다. 그 삽입어구[절] 이후에 나온 어구가 B일 것으로 예상하고 연결되는 A를 찾아 문맥으로 확인한다.

284 Organizations need to invest in data mining techniques to uncover hidden patterns, discover new knowledge, and as a consequence gain more insight into the current business situation. –사관학교응용

*data mining 데이터 마이닝 ((대규모 자료에서 새로운 정보를 찾아내는 일))

QUESTION 위 문장에서 and가 연결하고 있는 부분에 밑줄을 그으시오.

✳ **Error Points** 등위접속사 뒤의 삽입어구 앞뒤에 콤마가 없을 경우, 이 삽입어구를 병렬 대상인 B로 착각하지 않도록 주의한다.

285 Money when earned doing something you have a passion for will always bring you happiness and joy, and in more cases than not when someone has a passion in something and there is a market for it they become rich.

QUESTION 위 문장에서 and가 연결하고 있는 부분에 밑줄을 그으시오.

✳ **Advanced Points** 삽입어구 앞뒤에 콤마가 없는데 등위접속사까지 여러 개 겹쳐 나오면 문장 구조 파악이 매우 어려워지므로 문맥을 정확히 살펴야 한다.

286 If you take a closer look at your life, you may be able to find your life purpose — it could be as simple as raising a family, being a good friend, or emotionally encouraging others.

287 Make sure your wrists, forearms, and shoulders can stay relaxed while you work, and, this is important, keep in mind that even if you sit in the correct position, you'll still need to get up and stretch your body once in a while.

288 Deficiencies of innate ability may be compensated for through persistent hard work and concentration. One might say that work substitutes for talent, or better yet that it creates talent. —경찰대

289 Iron rusts from disuse; water loses its purity from stagnation and in cold weather becomes frozen; even so does action / inaction sap the vigor of the mind. —Leonardo da Vinci

*stagnation (액체가) 괴; 침체; 불경기 **sap 약화시키다, 차츰 무너뜨리다

QUESTION ▶ 위 문장의 네모 안에서 문맥에 맞는 낱말로 적절한 것을 고르시오.

290 It will not do to dismiss magic as nonsensical, because rationality is conditional in that the information available affects what is rational, and without modern science it was impossible for people to know what worked and what did not.

*nonsensical 터무니없는, 무의미한

291 In our day to day life we often come across some people who outwardly behave like friends but at difficult times of life play / plays a passive role or slowly disappear.

QUESTION ▶ 위 문장의 네모 안에서 어법상 적절한 것을 고르시오.

292 My parents having had a cup of green tea after every meal, I grew up on tea, and though I found it bitter at first came to enjoy it for its taste and health benefits.

293 Does Western culture always extinguish a local culture that buys into a Western way of doing things or on the other hand do the myriad pockets of local cultures around the world simultaneously receive and transform the Western commodities and styles in a way that _____ total homogenization?

*myriad 무수함, 많음 **homogenization 동질화

FILL-IN ▶ ① adopts ② resists

GOLDEN SAYING

It is not the man who has too little,
but the man who craves more,
that is poor.

-Seneca ((고대 로마 시인))

가난한 사람은 바로 너무 조금 가진 사람이 아니라, 더 많이 갈망하는 사람이다.

비교구문에서 정확히 이해해야 할 것들

Chapter Overview

● 비교구문을 포함한 문장은 as나 than 뒤에 흔히 생략이 일어나는데, 생략된 부분을 파악해야 정확하게 이해하고 해석할 수 있다.

● 서로 형태가 비슷한 비교구문들을 잘 구별하여 알아두어야 한다.

Chapter Goals

1 원급, 비교급, 최상급을 이용한 각 구문들의 의미를 말할 수 있다.

2 비교구문에서 생략된 어구를 파악할 수 있다.

3 형태상 혼동을 일으키는 비교급 구문의 종류와 의미를 말할 수 있다.

Must-know
Words &
Lexical
Phrases

UNIT 29 •⋯⋯⋯⋯⋯⋯⋯⋯⋯⋯⋯⋯⋯⋯⋯⋯

294 **magnify** 확대하다; 과장하다

   atom 원자

   cf. **atomic** 원자의; 원자력의

295 **pull up** 차를 세우다

   streamlined 간소화된, 능률화 된

296 **sustainable** 지속 가능한

   cf. **sustain** 지속하다; (무게, 고난을) 견디다

   alleviation 완화, 경감

   cf. **alleviate** 완화하다

297 **exclusivity** 배타성; 독점, 독점권

   (↔inclusivity 포용성, 포용책)

   cf. **exclusive** 배타적인; 독점적인 (↔inclusive 포괄적인, 폭넓은)

298 **regulate** 조절하다

   mammal 포유류

   alert 정신이 초롱초롱한, 기민한; 경계하는; 경계(시키다)

   confront 직면하다

299 **gravity** 중력 (=gravitational force)

   cf. **gravitational** 중력의

300 **overwhelm** 압도하다; 제압하다

   cf. **overwhelming** 압도적인, 엄청난

303 **psychosocial** 심리 사회적인

   let go of ~을 버리다, (손에서) 놓다 (=release); 포기하다

   get hold of ~을 구하다[찾다]; ~을 이해하다

304 **collision** 충돌

   cf. **collide** 충돌하다; 상충하다

   asteroid 소행성

   potential 가능성, 잠재력; 가능성이 있는, 잠재적인

   disastrous 파괴적인; 재난을 일으키는; 비참한

   peripheral 지엽적인, 주변적인

UNIT 30 •⋯⋯⋯⋯⋯⋯⋯⋯⋯⋯⋯⋯⋯⋯⋯⋯

305 **innovation** 혁신; 획기적인 것

   cf. **innovate** 혁신하다; (새로운 것을) 들여오다

diversity 다양성 (=variety)

cf. biodiversity 생물 다양성

306 classify 분류[구분]하다

307 pronoun ((문법)) 대명사

preposition ((문법)) 전치사

sequence 연속; 순서; 결과; 나열하다

308 constantly 끊임없이, 계속

consistent 일관된, 한결같은 (↔inconsistent 일관성 없는)

rationale 원리, 근본적 이유

309 isolation 고립, 격리, 분리

cf. isolate 고립시키다, 격리하다

profound 심각한; 깊은, 심오한

considerable 상당한, 많은

ⓘ considerate 사려 깊은, 배려하는

312 acid 산; 신맛이 나는 (것); 산성의; 신랄한

vessel 용기, 그릇, 통; (대형) 선박

314 discard (불필요한 것을) 폐기하다, 버리다

stand a chance 가능성이 있다

UNIT 31 •

315 knowledgeable 많이 아는, 아는 것이 많은

mundane 일상적인

plumbing 배관 작업; 수도 시설

carpentry 목공, 목수일

possess 소유하다; (특징을) 지니다

316 challenging 힘든; 도전 의식을 북돋우는

disciplined 통제가 잘 된, 훈련된

cf. discipline 규율; 훈육(하다); 징계

317 benefit 이득(을 보다)

cf. beneficial 이로운, 유익한

stimulating 자극을 주는

318 carry over (다른 상황에서 계속) 이어지다

multitude 다수; 대중, 군중

319 ensure 보장하다; 반드시 ~하게 하다

exercise (권리 등을) 행사하다; 운동(하다); 연습

secure 지키다; 확보하다; 안전한

320 proportion 비율; 부분; 크기; 균형

321 official 공무원, 관리; 공무상의; 공식적인

crack 균열; 갈라지다, 금이 가다

323 persist (일을) 계속하다, 지속하다

encounter 맞닥뜨리다

324 assure 보장하다; 확인하다; 장담하다, 확신하다

end result 최종 결과

imprison 구속하다; 감금하다

325 hypothetical 가상적인, 가정[가설]의

cf. hypothesis 가정, 가설, 추측

drastically 훨씬; 철저히, 과감하게; 급격히

UNIT 32 •

327 aid 도움

329 assimilate (음식, 지식 등을) 소화[흡수]하다;
(국가, 사회의 일원으로) 동화하다

330 enhance 향상시키다, 강화하다

331 predictor 예측 변수

334 mystify 혼란스럽게 하다; 속이다

335 perishable 상하기 쉬운

cf. perish 없어지다; 죽다

dairy 유제품의; 낙농(의)

canning 통조림 제조[가공]

ubiquity 보편성, 어디에나 존재함

336 restriction 제한, 규제

cf. restrict 제한하다, 통제하다

consume 먹다, 마시다; (에너지를) 소모하다

conserve 보존[보호]하다

significantly 상당히, 크게; 의미 있게

cf. significant 의미 있는, 중요한

hinder 방해하다; 저해하다

UNIT 29 비교구문

294 If a drop of water were magnified to the size of the world, the atoms in it would be about as large _____ baseballs.

QUESTION 위 문장의 빈칸에 알맞은 말을 쓰시오.

295 For those who need only a few items, it is far more reasonable to pull up to a highly streamlined convenience store _____ to run to a supermarket.

QUESTION 위 문장의 빈칸에 알맞은 말을 쓰시오.

296 Water is the most essential resource for economic growth, sustainable development or the alleviation of poverty worldwide of all the resources.

= No other resource is so essential for ~ worldwide as water is.

= No other resource is _____ _____ for ~ worldwide than water is.

= Water is more essential for ~ worldwide _____ _____ _____ resource.

QUESTION 위 문장의 빈칸에 알맞은 말을 쓰시오.

▽ Basic Points

1. 원급 표현: A as 형용사/부사 as B (A는 B만큼 ~하다)

• A not as[so] ~ as B	A는 B만큼 ~하지는 않다 (A⟨B)
• A 배수사 + as ~ as B (half, twice, three times, 분수 등)	A는 B보다 몇 배 ~하다
• as ~ as + S′ + can	가능한 한 ~한[하게] (= as ~ as possible)

2. 비교급 표현: A 비교급 ~ than B (A는 B보다 더 ~하다)

• A 배수사 + 비교급 than B	A는 B보다 몇 배 ~하다
• the + 비교급 ~, the + 비교급 ...	~하면 할수록 더욱 ...하다
• 부정문, much[still, even] less ~	~은커녕, (~이 아님은) 말할 것도 없이 (= let alone)
• the + 비교급 ~ of the two ...	두 ... 중에 더 ~한 쪽

3. 최상급 표현: A 최상급 ~+of 복수명사[in 단수명사] (A는 ...에서 가장 ~하다)

- 부정어 ~ as[so] 원급 ~ (as A)
- 부정어 ~ 비교급 ~ than A
- A 비교급 ~ than any other

297 Exclusivity in problem solving, even with a genius, is not as effective as inclusivity, where everyone's ideas are heard and a solution is developed through collaboration. —모의응용

298 Yawning may be one of the most important mechanisms for regulating survival-related behavior in mammals. So if you want to stay alert and active, yawn as many times a day as possible — especially when you're confronting a difficult problem at work and when you feel anger, anxiety or stress. −모의응용

299 There is gravity on the moon, but the gravitational force is much weaker than the earth's. Thus, objects on the moon weigh one-sixth as much as they do on the earth. −모의응용

300 The less willing you are to share your problems with loved ones and friends, the more those problems will come to overwhelm you.

301 Certainly it should be clear that the more science we possess, the more philosophy we need, because the more power we have, the more direction we need.

302 If you are not exposed to many types of books, you will not develop a true appreciation for reading, much less the skills necessary to become a great writer.

303 Erik Erikson, well-known for his psychosocial development theory, emphasizes that no factor is as important as trust in the child's developing personality. According to him, basic trust involves having the courage to _____ the familiar and take a step toward the unknown. −수능응용

FILL-IN ① let go of ② get hold of

304 Except for nuclear war or a collision with an asteroid, no force has more potential to damage our planet's web of life than global warming.

*web of life 생물망 ((생명체의 존재가 거미줄처럼 서로 연관됨을 나타내는 말))

SUMMARY Global warming could be the most disastrous / peripheral for life of our planet.

as ~, than ~ 이하의 반복어구 생략

305 As a source of exchange, innovation and creativity, cultural diversity is as necessary for humankind as biodiversity is for nature.

> QUESTION 위 문장에서 생략이 일어난 곳에 ✔ 표시하고 생략된 어구를 쓰시오.

🌿 **Main Points** 원급 표현의 두 번째 as와 비교급 표현의 than 뒤에서 앞의 내용이 반복될 때, 반복되는 어구는 거의 생략된다. 생략된 어구를 보충하여 생각하면 좀 더 이해가 쉬워진다.

306 Unsurprisingly, people who used the internet daily were much more likely than those classified as 'light users' to feel informed about international news.

> QUESTION 위 문장에서 생략이 일어난 곳에 ✔ 표시하고 생략된 어구를 쓰시오.

✳ **Advanced Points** 원급 표현의 두 번째 as 뒤 또는 비교급 표현의 than 뒤의 비교 대상이 앞으로 이동하는 경우가 종종 있다. 두 번째 as 또는 than 바로 앞으로 이동한 비교 대상을 찾아서 구조를 확인한 후에, 생략된 어구를 보충해 본다.
위의 예문의 경우, than 앞의 어구인 be likely는 뒤쪽의 to feel ~과 연결되는 것이며, 비교 대상(those classified as 'light users')이 비교급 가까이로 이동한 것이다. (→ people ~ were much more likely *to feel informed* ~ than those classified ~.)

307 In the language of dance, connecting steps are as important to ballet as pronouns and prepositions are to a sentence. Without them, all you are left with is a series of poses, not a sequence of movement.

308 Companies that change constantly but without any consistent rationale will collapse just as ⬚sure / surely⬚ as those that change not at all. −모의

> QUESTION 위 문장의 네모 안에서 어법상 적절한 것을 고르시오.

309 Britain was attached to Europe during the last Ice Age and remains close to Europe, and consequently its isolation is not as profound as <u>that</u> of New Zealand, which is a considerable distance from the nearest continent.

> QUESTION 문장의 밑줄 친 that이 가리키는 것을 적으시오.

310 When a person lies, their responses will come more slowly because the brain needs more time to process the details of a new invention than to recall stored facts. – 모의응용

311 You can make more friends in two months by becoming interested in other people than you can in two years by trying to get other people interested in you. – Dale Carnegie ((美 작가))

SUMMARY▶ Showing interest in others is an effective / ineffective way to make friends.

312 Anger is an acid that can do more harm to the vessel in which it is stored than to anything on which it is poured. – Mark Twain ((美 소설가))

313 Greenwashing is the activity that makes people believe that a company is doing more to protect the environment than it really is by taking an existing product and spinning its environmentally-friendly virtues even if there are none.

*spin (정보를 그럴듯하게) 제시하다

314 While most newspapers are discarded after a day, magazines can be kept for months, and are often widely shared, which means that ads in magazines stand a better chance than newspaper ads of being seen and remembered.

315 There are people who are knowledgeable about mundane things — plumbing, carpentry, or baseball, for example — but intellectuals who possess lots of knowledge about academic topics tend to be more commonly called "knowledgeable."

> **QUESTION** 위 문장의 밑줄 친 부분에서 생략된 than 이하를 쓰시오.

🌿 **Main Points** as나 than 뒤의 비교 대상이 생략되어 있을 경우 생략된 것이 무엇인지를 보충하여 생각하면 이해가 좀 더 쉬워진다. A와 B를 비교할 때 비교 대상 B를 than과 함께 통째로 생략하는 이유는 대개 다음과 같다.
1. 밝히지 않아도 문맥상 명백한 경우
2. 앞 내용에서 이미 밝혀진 경우
3. 과거 vs. 현재, 현재 vs. 미래 등 시간상의 비교

316 From now on, telecommuting or self-study will be more common in our lifestyle. Remaining energized and motivated can be more challenging without a support system, but it can be achieved with planning and disciplined action.

> **QUESTION** 위 문장의 밑줄 친 부분에서 생략된 than 이하를 쓰시오.

❋ **Advanced Points** A와 B를 비교할 때, 생략된 비교 대상 B는 생략되지 않은 A와 대조되는 내용일 수도 있다. 위 예문에서 두 번째 문장의 than 이하는 A와 대조되는 내용으로, 문맥상 명백하여 통째로 생략되었다.

317 Against the background of home schooling gaining in popularity, many studies have shown that students benefit more in a classroom setting since the interaction with other students creates a stimulating learning environment. –사관학교응용

318 Although the American is not comfortable with long periods of silence in the conversation, the Asian will take time to answer. This can carry over into the classroom, as the English learner from other cultures may be slower to answer for a multitude of reasons, such as thinking of how to translate or cultural conversational style.

319 We need more effective ways to ensure that every citizen can fully exercise the right to secure private information. −수능

320 As you grow and become a nicer person, your relationships should grow and improve as well, and in the same proportion.

321 If officials had made the right decision when the cracks were first found in the building, the collapse might have been prevented, or at least managed better.

322 One of the effects of aging is that your body becomes less able to regulate its temperature in such a way that you are unable to properly judge if you are warm or cold. −모의응용

323 Supposing we have a high sense of self-confidence, <u>we will set higher goals, be less afraid of failure, and persist longer when we encounter difficulties.</u>

−경찰대응용

QUESTION 위 문장의 밑줄 친 부분에서 생략된 than 이하에 해당되는 내용을 완성하시오.
than when we don't _____

324 Our happiness and our free self-expression is much more assured if we let go of end results; work toward your goals and don't be imprisoned by them.

−모의응용

325 If we lived in a society with no hypothetical situations, our society might be drastically less advanced; human imagination and creativity are the foundation on which science and technology can be explored.

SUMMARY The major source of progress is the ability to [imagine / explore].

326 The increases in skill and technology themselves <u>have ensured no more increase in human happiness or well-being than academic development has.</u>

> QUESTION 위 문장에서 밑줄 친 부분과 같은 의미가 되도록 다음 빈칸에 적절한 것을 쓰시오.
> have not ensured an increase in human happiness or well-being _____ _____ _____ academic development has

🌿 **Main Points**

- not so much A as B = not A so much as B: A라기보다는 오히려 B (= B rather than A)
  cf. not so much as ~: ~조차도 아니다[없다], ~와 같은 그 정도도 아니다 (= not even)

- A no more ~ than B = A not ~ any more than B: A는 B와 마찬가지로 ~ 아니다 (A=B, than 앞뒤를 모두 부정),
  B가 아닌 것처럼 A도 ~ 아니다
- A no less ~ than B = A just as ~ as B: A는 꼭 B만큼 ~하다 (A=B, than 앞뒤를 모두 긍정),
  B가 ~인 것처럼 A도 그렇다

〈no + 비교급 + than〉 = 〈as + 반대 의미 원급 + as〉
- no more than ~ = as few/little as ~ = only ~: 겨우 ~인
- no less than ~ = as many/much as ~: ~나 되는

다음 구문들은 주로 뒤에 수나 양에 해당하는 표현을 동반한다.
- not more than ~ = at most ~: 많아야, 기껏해야
- not less than ~ = at least ~: 적어도

327 It is important, not so much <u>to give a man bread</u>, as to put him in the way of earning it for himself; not to give direct aid, but to help others to help themselves.

> QUESTION 위 문장에서 밑줄 친 to give a man bread가 의미하는 바를 찾아서 밑줄을 그으시오.

328 A year after the historic tornado outbreak, the unusually quiet weather has resulted in a somewhat peaceful spring. There was not so much as a single tornado warning issued by the weather service.

329 Thinking is a natural thing, just like breathing or nutrition. This means that we do not learn to think any more than we learn to breathe or to assimilate food.

330 Researchers have recognized that laughter is no less _____ than exercise in terms of enhancing our physical and mental performance. Laughing can create significant hormonal changes in the body, ultimately helping it resist disease, and in some cases curing it.

FILL-IN ① beneficial ② harmful

331 Surprisingly, despite the enormous opportunities in a family for exposing children to the foods eaten by the parents, parental preferences are weak predictors of child food preferences; in fact, they are no better predictors than the preferences of other adults. −경찰대

332 Having knowledge but lacking the power to express it clearly is no better than never having any ideas at all. −Pericles ((고대 그리스 정치인))

333 To encourage student participation in group discussion, it is recommended to involve no more than 20 persons and to plan the material to be covered carefully.

334 Many phenomena mystify the human mind, and when people do not have scientific explanations they will construct other explanations that, no less than the former, influence their conduct. −경찰대응용

QUESTION 위 문장의 밑줄 친 the former가 의미하는 바를 찾아 밑줄을 그으시오.

335 People can enjoy perishable foods like fruits, vegetables, and dairy products, previously storable for not more than a month, for up to six months of the year, due to the invention of canning and the ubiquity of fridges.

336 While on a diet, you should eat less, but not less than 1,200 calories, since extreme restriction of consumed calories sends signals to your body to conserve calories, which can significantly slow your metabolic rate, and hinder / help your weight loss goals. *metabolic 신진대사의

QUESTION 위 문장의 네모 안에서 문맥에 맞는 낱말로 적절한 것을 고르시오.

REVIEW: CHAPTER08

A와 B의 비교 결과 총정리

1 A=B (A와 B가 서로 같음)

A as ~ as B	A는 B만큼 ~하다
A no less ~ than B	A는 꼭 B만큼 ~하다, B가 ~인 것처럼 A도 ~이다
A no more ~ than B	A는 B와 마찬가지로 ~ 아니다. A가 ~아닌 것은 B가 ~이 아닌 것과 같다

2 A〉B 또는 A≧B (A가 B보다 정도가 더하거나 같음)

A -er[more ~] than B	A는 B보다 더 ~하다
A not less ~ than B	A는 B 못지않게 (그 이상으로) ~이다 (A≧B)
A 배수사(two times ...) as ~ as B	A는 B의 …배만큼 ~하다
A 배수사(two times ...) than B	A는 B보다 …배 더 ~하다
A rather than B	B라기보다는 오히려 A이다

3 A〈B 또는 A≦B (A가 B보다 정도가 덜하거나 같음)

A less ~ than B	A는 B만큼 ~하지 않다
A not as[so] ~ as B	
not so much A as B	
not A so much as B	A라기보다는 오히려 B이다
B rather than A	
A not more ~ than B	(A와 B 모두 ~이긴 하지만) A는 B만큼 ~인 것은 아니다 (A≦B)
A 배수사(half ...) as ~ as B	A는 B의 …배만큼 ~하다

CHAPTER

09

아는 것 같지만
한 번 더 생각해야 하는 구문

Chapter Overview

- it, they, this, that의 경우, 대명사, 가주어, 연결사 등 여러 쓰임 중 어느 용도로 사용되었는지 판단하는 것이 쉽지 않다. it의 경우, 문장 뒤쪽에 to-v, that ~이 있어도 가주어가 아닌 대명사일 수 있으므로 문맥을 잘 살펴야 한다.

- 문장에 과거형 조동사 would, could 등이 있으면 '가정'하는 내용이 숨어 있는 가정법이 아닐지 생각해 봐야 한다.

- 부정어(구)들은 자칫 놓치면 문장의 의미를 정반대로 이해하게 되므로 매우 주의해야 한다. 특히 부정부사는 빈칸, 요약문, 밑줄 함의 추론 등의 문제에서 함정으로 활용되므로, 의미를 정확히 알아야 한다.

- 인과나 선후 관계를 나타내는 동사들이 수동태로 쓰일 때 의미 관계를 혼동하지 않도록 주의해야 한다.

Chapter Goals

1 문맥을 살펴서 it, they, this, that이 대명사인지 확인하고, 그것이 가리키는 것을 판단할 수 있다.

2 if절의 의미를 포함할 수 있는 어구 네 가지를 나열할 수 있다.

3 부정어구가 이루는 구문을 정확히 해석할 수 있다.

4 인과/선후를 나타내는 동사가 수동태로 쓰인 경우 원인과 결과, 먼저와 나중의 순서를 혼동하지 않고 구별할 수 있다.

U N I T 3 3 •

337 **enterprise** (대규모) 사업; 기업, 회사; 진취성

undertake 시작하다; 맡다, 책임지다; 약속하다

conclusively 단호히, 결정적으로

cf. conclusive 결정적인, 확실한

338 **selfish** 이기적인

instinctively 본능적으로

cf. instinct 본능

instinctive 본능적인, 직감에 따른

339 **resilience** (충격, 부상 등에서의) 회복력; 탄성, 탄력

cf. resilient 회복력 있는; 탄력 있는

put together 조합하여 만들다, 조립하다

340 **garment** 옷, 의복

launder 세탁하다

cf. laundry 세탁물

341 **keep up with** (유행을) 따르다; ~에 뒤지지 않다

343 **hydrate** 수분을 공급하다

344 **constructive** 건설적인 (↔destructive 파괴적인)

345 **primitive** 원시의, 원시적인

specialized 전문적인, 전문화된

cf. specialize 전공하다, 전문적으로 다루다

transmit 전달하다, 전송하다; 전염시키다; (열, 전기 등을) 전도하다

cf. transmission 전송; 전염; 전도

enact 일어나다, 벌어지다; (법을) 제정하다; (연극을) 상연하다

institution 기관, 단체; 제도

346 **infection** 감염; 전염병

347 **enrich** 풍요롭게 하다; 부유하게 하다

U N I T 3 4 •

348 **consumption** 소비

accompany (일, 현상 등이) 동반되다; (사람과) 동행하다

proportional 비례하는

livestock 가축

emission 배출(물); 배기가스

cf. emit 내뿜다

349 **recession** 불황 (=depression); 후퇴

    job hunting 구직 활동

350 **fraction** 조금, 소량; 파편, 부분; ((수학)) 분수

351 **shortage** 부족

    breakdown 붕괴, 몰락

    mass production 대량 생산

352 **comprehend** 이해하다

    cf. **comprehensive** 포괄적인

        comprehensible 이해할 수 있는

    thorough 철저한, 완전한; 뛰어난

    proficient 능숙한, 숙련된

353 **imprudent** 경솔한 (=rash)

    intuition 직관(력), 직감

    cf. **intuitive** 직관에 의한; 직관력이 있는

355 **wander** 거닐다, 돌아다니다

    plain 평원, 평지; 분명한; 솔직한; 무늬가 없는; 쉬운

356 **appreciate** 인정하다, 진가를 알아보다; 감상하다; 감사하다

357 **televise** (텔레비전으로) 방송하다

    trial 재판; 실험; 시련

    come forward (도움을 주겠다고) 나서다

UNIT 35

361 **variation** 편차, 차이; 변화, 변형

    cf. **vary** 다르다; 바뀌다

        varied 다양한, 다채로운

    excel 우수하다, 뛰어나다, 탁월하다

    pursue (방침 등에) 따르다; ~을 뒤쫓다

362 **mindful** 신경을 쓰는, 주의하는, 유념하는

363 **rational** 합리적인; 이성적인

364 **sponsor** 후원하다; 후원자

    be associated with ~와 연관되다

365 **amusing** 재미있는, 즐거운

    strikingly 두드러지게, 현저히

    cf. **striking** 돋보이는, 현저한

    companion 친구; 동료

366 **adequate** 충분한, 적절한

370 **subsist** 먹고살다, 생활하다; 존속되다, 유효하다

    foraging 수렵 채집

UNIT 36 •

372 **superstitious** 미신을 믿는, 미신적인

    reinforcement 강화

    cf. **reinforce** 강화하다, 보강하다

373 **legitimation** 인정; 정당화; 합법화

    cf. **legitimate** 정당한; 합법적인

    discourse 이야기, 담화

374 **mandatory** 의무적인, 법에 정해진 (=obligatory, compulsory)

    A contribute to B A가 B의 원인이 되다

    tempt 부추기다, 유혹하다

    cf. **tempt A to-v** A가 v하도록 부추기다

376 **longevity** 수명; 장수

377 **transition** (다른 상태로의) 변화, 이행(移行)

    hunter-gatherer 수렵 채집인

    establishment 확립; 시설

    domestication 사육, 길들이기

378 **precede** 앞서다, 먼저 일어나다

    arch 아치(형 구조물); (몸을) 구부리다

379 **mortality** 사망(률); 죽음을 피할 수 없음

380 **iconic** 우상의; 상징이 되는; 전통적인

    legacy 유산

대명사 it, they, this, that

337 It is likely that any major enterprise that was ever undertaken had an expert arguing conclusively that <u>it</u> would not succeed.

QUESTION 위 문장에서 밑줄 친 it이 가리키는 것을 찾아 밑줄을 그으시오.

🖋 **Main Points** 대명사 it, they, this, these, that, those 등은 문맥을 살펴 그것이 나타내는 수에 따라 앞에서 그와 일치하는 수의 명사를 찾도록 한다.

338 Speaking of rudeness, to be rude is not just to be selfish, in the way that children (until taught otherwise) and animals are instinctively selfish; <u>it</u> is a decision to ignore others that results in being alone. —모의응용

QUESTION 위 문장에서 밑줄 친 it이 가리키는 것을 찾아 밑줄을 그으시오.

✳ **Error Points** 대명사 it을 뒤에 나오는 to부정사구나 that절을 대신하는 가주어나 가목적어로 혼동하지 않도록 한다.

339 Resilience is accepting your new reality, even if it's less good than the one you had before. You can fight it, you can do nothing but scream about what you've lost, or you can accept that and try to put together something that's good. —Elizabeth Edwards ((美 변호사))

340 Should you put a very dirty garment into a washing machine with other clothes, it may cause all the garments to be muddy-looking after they have been laundered.

341 People who are very interested in keeping up with the latest fashion trends will not wear the clothes that they bought last year, even though those are still in perfect condition.

342 Leadership requires the skill to be a cause for positive change by doing the right thing at the right time and this is what makes a person capable of being a leader.

343 Temperatures tend to be at their highest between 10 a.m. to 2 p.m., so that is a good time to avoid being outside to stay hydrated during hot weather, and <u>this</u> will keep you from getting heat stroke.

*heat stroke 열사병

QUESTION 위 문장에서 밑줄 친 this가 가리키는 것을 고르시오.
① the highest temperature between 10 to 2   ② to avoid being outside to stay hydrated

344 We often forget that the main purpose of criticizing is not to be negative but to be constructive: to fix something. But general criticism is destructive, and it doesn't lead anyone to know how to fix things; it just makes people feel bad.

345 Unlike the modern society, the primitive society had less specialized knowledge to transmit, and since its way of life was enacted before the eyes of all, it had no need to create a separate institution of education, such as the school. – 수능응용

346 Medical waste holds risk for infection, so <u>it</u> has to be handled with special methods to prevent a biological risk from being introduced to the environment or community.

QUESTION 위 문장에서 밑줄 친 it이 가리키는 것을 고르시오.
① medical waste   ② infection

347 Only true acting can completely absorb an audience, making <u>it</u> not only understand but participate emotionally in all that is transpiring on the stage, thus enriching the audience with an inner experience that will not be erased by time.

*transpire 일어나다, 발생하다

QUESTION 위 문장에서 밑줄 친 it이 가리키는 것을 고르시오.
① true acting   ② an audience

Plus⁺ paraphrasing(패러프레이징, 바꾸어 표현하기)

앞서 나온 말을 대명사가 아닌 다른 어구로 바꾸어 표현하는 경우도 자주 있다.

Even traditional holidays such as Christmas are these days mainly about consumption. **What was originally a religious holiday** has been overtaken by acts of consumption, such as gift giving. – 사관학교응용

크리스마스와 같은 전통적인 휴일조차도 요즘에는 주로 소비와 관련된다. **원래 종교적인 휴일이었던 것**(= 크리스마스)은 선물 주기와 같은 소비 활동에 잠식 당했다.

348 Lower consumption of meat and dairy products accompanied by a proportional reduction in livestock production would reduce greenhouse gas emissions as well as the area of land use.

QUESTION 위 문장에서 if절의 의미를 포함하는 부분을 찾아 밑줄을 그으시오.

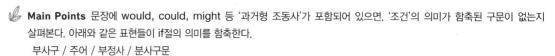

Main Points 문장에 would, could, might 등 '과거형 조동사'가 포함되어 있으면, '조건'의 의미가 함축된 구문이 없는지 살펴본다. 아래와 같은 표현들이 if절의 의미를 함축한다.
부사구 / 주어 / 부정사 / 분사구문
이 외에 otherwise(그렇지 않다면), without, but for(~이 없(었)다면) 등이 if절을 대신하기도 한다.

349 In a normal year without recession, students would have successfully finished their job hunting while still in their final year of university.

QUESTION 위 문장이 뜻하는 바로 적절한 것을 고르시오.
① 경제 불황으로 학생들이 직장을 구하기 어려웠다.
② 경제가 활성화되어 학생들이 취업을 서두르지 않았다.

350 <u>Just a fraction nearer the sun</u>, the Earth would be a furnace like Venus, considering the temperature of the sun, which is around 6,000°C.

*furnace 몹시 뜨거운 곳; 용광로

QUESTION 위 문장에서 밑줄 친 부분과 일치하는 의미의 문장을 완성하시오. (주어진 단어 활용 가능)
= _____ it (be) _____ just a fraction nearer the sun

351 Industrial diamonds are so important that a shortage would cause a breakdown in the metalworking industry and would destroy mass production. – 수능응용

*metalworking 금속 세공

352 An intelligent person would have comprehended that the perfect singing of the singer was not due to natural gifts alone. The singer had received a thorough training, and, though young, she was very proficient.

353 It would be imprudent, not to say foolish, to rely on your instincts and intuition all the time.

354 The quickest way to enjoy your hobby more is to make it a job. To turn a hobby into a business would give you the passion to truly enjoy your work.

355 Invented 10,000 years earlier, the camera could have recorded mammoths wandering the plains during the last Ice Age.

356 Recognized by a wider audience, Franz Kafka might have been appreciated during his time, but the author died from tuberculosis at age 40, before much of his work was published or even finished.　　　*tuberculosis 결핵

357 It is necessary to televise trials to increase the chance of a fair trial. If trials are televised, a huge audience will be made aware of cases, and crucial witnesses who would otherwise be ignorant of a case may come forward.

－모의응용

358 The recent spirit of cooperation among various branches of the sciences has led to a number of discoveries which <u>otherwise</u> might not have been made.

QUESTION 위 문장에서 밑줄 친 부분 otherwise가 뜻하는 바로 적절한 것을 고르시오.
① if there had not been the spirit of cooperation among various branches of science
② if there have not been a number of discoveries of science

359 Probably unconsciously, primitive hunters had moved from Asia across the land bridge to hunt animals and become the first immigrants to the new land. Without the ice age, North America might have remained unpopulated for thousands of years more. －모의응용

360 What keeps all of the scholars going when things are going badly is their passion for their academic work. But for passion, they would achieve nothing.

－모의응용

361 Since there are variations among students in their school performance and in their potential to excel academically, <u>not all students pursue the same course of academic training.</u>

> QUESTION ▶ 위 문장의 밑줄 친 부분과 같은 의미가 되도록 다음 네모 안에서 적절한 것을 고르시오.
> = ☐ Some / None ☐ of the students pursue a different course of academic training.

362 It is important to be mindful about every single aspect of purchasing food. Try not to race through your shopping. In my hometown, <u>nobody would buy a melon without feeling it and smelling it;</u> and nobody would dream of buying a chicken without knowing which farm it came from and what it ate. –수능

> QUESTION ▶ 위 문장의 밑줄 친 부분과 같은 의미가 되도록 다음 네모 안에서 적절한 것을 고르시오.
> = ☐ All / Some ☐ people would buy a melon after feeling it and smelling it.

 Main Points

1. 부분부정
   - not all[every, both, always, necessarily, altogether, entirely, ...]: 모두[전부, 둘 다, 항상, 반드시, 다 합쳐서, 전적으로, ...] ~한 것은 아니다
   - A, it does not follow that B: A라고 해서 반드시 B인 것은 아니다

2. 이중부정: 부정어(구)+부정어(구) = 강한 긍정
   하나의 문장에 부정을 나타내는 표현이 두 개 있으면 부정의 의미가 사라지고 강한 긍정의 의미가 된다.
   - 부정어 A without B: A하면 반드시 B 한다

3. 부정어(not, never, no 등)가 포함되어 있지 않으면서도 부정의 뜻을 나타내는 어구
   - far from: 전혀 ~ 아닌; ~와는 거리가 먼
   - free from: ~이 없는; ~을 면한
   - beyond: ~이 미치지 않는, ~할 수 없는
   - be[have] yet to-v: 아직 v하지 않고 있다[않았다]
   - lest[for fear]+S'(+should)+V': V하지 않도록 (= so that+S'+may not+V'); V할까 봐
   - anything but: ~이 결코 아닌
   - the last ~ to-v: 결코 v할 것 같지 않은 ~
   - above: ~하지 않는; ~을 초월한

   이외에, 반어적인 의미를 나타내는 의문문, 즉 긍정의문문이 부정의 뜻을, 부정의문문이 긍정의 뜻을 나타내는 경우에 유의해야 한다. (수사의문문)
   Who doesn't know we have to pursue our passion to have a rewarding career?
   보람 있는 직업을 갖기 위해 열정을 추구해야 함을 **누가 모르겠는가**? (= **Everyone knows** we have to pursue ~)

363 Just because you are intelligent or have great knowledge does not mean you can think critically. Critical thinking is about how we use our intelligence and knowledge to reach objective and rational viewpoints.

※ **Advanced Points** not과 because가 쓰인 문장의 해석에 주의하자. 양보의 의미로, 아래와 같이 해석해야 한다.
   - (just[only]) because ~ not ...: ~이라고 해서 ...은 아니다 (= not ... because ~)

364 Because a man has his faults, it does not follow that what he has produced, sponsored or been associated with is worthless. Likewise, because a man is beyond praise, it does not follow that his every idea is so good that it doesn't need to be examined.

365 The age of 3½ is <u>not without its charm</u>. One of the more amusing aspects of this age is the child's often vivid imagination, which is expressed most strikingly in their enjoyment of imaginary companions. – 수능응용

> QUESTION ▶ 위 문장에서 밑줄 친 <u>not without its charm</u>이 의미하는 바로 적절한 것을 고르시오.
> ① doesn't have any appeal   ② has its own appeal

366 In less developed countries, the quality and scale of secondary education are far from adequate and need to be reformed in order to meet the UN's universal education target.

367 Futurists agree that schooling needs to prepare students for jobs that don't exist yet, to work with tools that have yet to be created, and to solve problems that have yet to be identified.

368 Over the past couple of years we have seen an explosion in social media, and now it seems everyone is rushing to jump on the bandwagon for fear that they be left out of the opportunities that it can offer.

*jump on the bandwagon 유행에 합류하다

369 What does it matter if we have a new book or an old book, if we open neither? – Jesse Jackson ((美 정치인))

> QUESTION ▶ 위 문장이 의미하는 바로 적절한 것을 고르시오.
> ① How old the good book is doesn't matter.   ② What matters is whether you read the book or not.

370 People in the world today who subsist by hunting, fishing and gathering plants are not following an ancient way of life because they do not know any better; they are doing it either because they have been forced by circumstances into a situation where foraging is the best means of survival or because they simply prefer to live this way.

371 ① <u>Some changes in the environment</u> have been caused by ② <u>natural events</u>; many more are the result of things that people have done.

QUESTION 위 문장에서 밑줄 친 ①과 ② 중, '결과'를 고르시오.

372 Superstitious behavior is the result of people believing that when ① <u>specific activities</u> are followed by ② <u>rewards</u>, they are the cause of the positive reinforcement, even though this may not be true.

QUESTION 위 문장에서 밑줄 친 ①과 ② 중, '먼저 일어난 일'을 고르시오.

🖋 **Main Points** 인과관계를 나타내는 동사가 수동태로 쓰인 경우, 원인과 결과를 서로 혼동하지 않도록 해야 한다.

- A be ⎡ caused ⎤ by B
⎢ brought about ⎢
⎣ accounted for ⎦

- A be ⎡ attributed ⎤ to B
⎣ ascribed ⎦

→ A는 B 때문이다. A의 원인(이유)은 B에 있다 (A: 결과, B: 원인)

마찬가지로, 선후관계를 나타내는 동사가 수동태로 쓰인 경우에도 앞뒤의 일을 혼동하지 않도록 주의한다.
- A **be followed[accompanied] by** B   A에 뒤이어 B가 오다 (A → B)
- A **be preceded by** B   A에 앞서 B가 오다 (B → A)
- A **be survived by** B   A는 B를 (유족으로) 남겨두고 먼저 죽다

373 The great explosion of scientific creativity in sixteenth-century Europe was certainly helped by the sudden spread of information brought about by Gutenberg's use of movable type in printing and by the legitimation of everyday languages, which rapidly replaced Latin as the medium of discourse. ─모의

*movable type 가동 활자 ((낱낱으로 독립된 활자))

374 ① <u>The phenomenon</u> that safety measures, like mandatory wearing of seat belts, contribute to careless driving may be accounted for by ② <u>the notion</u> that a greater sense of security tempts people to take more risks. ─수능응용

QUESTION 위 문장에서 밑줄 친 ①과 ② 중, '결과'를 고르시오.

375 Before the modern scientific era, creativity was attributed to a superhuman force; all novel ideas originated with the gods. The Latin verb for "inspire" also means "breathe into," reflecting that creative inspiration was regarded as similar to God first breathing life into man. —모의응용

> **SUMMARY** Before modern times, people believed that all creativity resulted from / in the gods.

376 Some of the difference in longevity between species is ascribed to the degree to which they manufacture their own antioxidants, which absorb harmful materials before they cause damage to their bodies. *antioxidant 노화[산화] 방지제

377 In general, since the transition from hunter-gatherer lifestyles to farming, the establishment of agriculture has been accompanied by the domestication of cattle and other livestock.

> **QUESTION** 위 문장이 뜻하는 바로 적절한 것을 고르시오.
> ① 농업 정착에 뒤이어 가축을 사육하였다.
> ② 가축을 사육함으로 인해서 농업이 정착되었다.

378 While rainbows are often preceded by violent storms that might otherwise make us cold, wet, and uncomfortable, looking up afterward to see an incredibly colorful arch in the sky somehow makes us feel better.

379 When infant mortality rates are high, as they are in much of the developing world, parents tend to have high numbers of children to ensure that some will survive to adulthood. There has never been a sustained drop in birth rates that was not first preceded by a sustained drop in infant mortality. —경찰대

380 The musician is survived by his wife, children, and countless music fans across the world to whom his iconic legacy will live on forever.

Move Forward

구조·구문편 | 길고 복잡한 문장에 대처하라

많은 시간을 투자해 길고 복잡한 내용을 모두 빠짐없이 파악해야만 성공적인 독해를 했다고 볼 수는 없다.
아무리 길고 복잡한 내용이라도 분명하고 간단하게 정리하여 이해하는 능력이 더 중요하다.
때로는 건너뛰면서 핵심에 초점을 맞추고, 때로는 앞으로 전개될 내용을 예상하면서 정확성과 속도를 잡아보자!

과감히 건너뛰고 적극적으로 예측하라

Chapter Overview

● 영어에서 부연 설명에 해당하는 것들은 꼭 읽어야 하는 정보가 아닌 이상, 과감히 건너뛰어도 핵심을 이해하는 데는 문제가 없을 가능성이 크다. 특히, 부연 설명이 길고 복잡하다면 이를 굳이 읽고 이해하는 데 시간을 들일 필요는 없다.

● 읽은 내용을 바탕으로 앞으로 전개될 내용을 예측하면서 읽는 것이 정확성과 속도를 높이는 비결이다. 예측을 도와주는 신호어들을 적극적으로 이용해야 한다.

Chapter Goals

1 부연 설명을 이끄는 구문들을 문장에서 판별할 수 있다.

2 핵심 내용을 이해한 정도에 따라 부연 설명을 읽을지 건너뛸지를 결정할 수 있다.

3 앞으로 전개될 내용을 연결어와 신호어를 보고 예측할 수 있다.

Must-know
Words &
Lexical
Phrases

UNIT 37 •

381 susceptible (~에) 영향을 받기 쉬운; 민감한

  makeup 구성, 구조

  cf. make up ~을 이루다[구성하다]; 만들어 내다

382 herd (짐승의) 무리, 떼; 사람들, 대중

  ingenious 재주가 많은; 기발한, 독창적인

  ⓘ ingenuous 순진한, 사람을 잘 믿는

383 exemplify (전형적인) 예시가 되다; 예를 들다

385 bias 편향, 편견

  assume (사실이라고) 가정[추정]하다; ~인 체하다; (권력, 책임을) 맡다

  cf. assumption 가정, 가설, 억측

386 finding (조사, 연구 등의) 결과, 결론; (법정의) 판결

  guidance 지침, 지도, 안내

  inform A of B A에게 B를 알려주다

387 intimately 밀접하게, 깊이; 친밀하게

  cf. intimate 밀접한, 깊은; 친밀한; 사적인

  interconnect 서로 연결하다[관련되다]

  imperceptibly 알아차릴 수 없게, 미미하게

  cf. imperceptible 감지할 수 없는, 미세한, 경미한

  accumulate 축적되다, 쌓이다

388 underlying 근본적인, 근원적인

  conviction 확신, 신념; 유죄 판결

389 distort 왜곡하다; 비틀다, 일그러뜨리다

  warrant 뒷받침하다, 정당화하다; 보증; 증명서

390 elaborate 정교한, 정성을 들인; 자세히 설명하다

  mature 나이가 들다; 숙성시키다; 성숙한; 숙성된

UNIT 38 •

391 alliance 결합, 결연; 동맹, 연합

  arrangement 합의; 준비, 주선; 배열, 배치

  notion 개념, 관념, 생각

392 sculptor 조각가

  property ((주로 복수형)) 특성, 속성; 재산; 부동산

393 ritual 풍습, 관습; 의식, 의례(적인 일)

  restore 회복시키다; 복원하다

externally 외적으로 (↔internally 내적으로)

cf. **external** 외적인, 외부의; 외국의

394 **promote** 촉진하다, 향상시키다 (=encourage); 승진시키다; 홍보하다

consensus 의견 일치, 합의

upset (상황, 계획을) 어긋나게 하다, 망치다; 속상하게 하다; 속상한

395 **embody** 구체적으로 표현하다; 포함하다

396 **come out with** (상품을) 출시하다; (책을) 출판하다

defensive 방어적인 (태도의); 수비의 (↔offensive 공격적인)

odds (the -) 가능성; 역경, 곤란

offering (판매할) 제품 (의 제공); 공물, 제물

eat into (돈, 시간을) 거덜 내다; 침식[부식]시키다

397 **aroused** 흥분한

398 **hang out with** ~와 어울리다[시간을 보내다]

like-minded 뜻이 맞는, 같은 생각의

ideology 이념, 이데올로기; 관념

399 **aquatic** 수생의, 물에서 자라는; 물과 관련된

401 **overly** 지나치게, 몹시

zealous 열성적인

cognitive 인지의, 인식의

intrude 방해하다; 침범하다

UNIT 39 •

404 **array of** 다수의 ~; ~의 배열

405 **on the surface** 표면적으로, 보기에는

relate to A A를 이해하다[공감하다]; A와 관련되다

function ((수학)) 함수; 기능

406 **critique** 비평, 평론(하다)

argumentation 논증

mechanism (정해진) 방법, 절차; 구조, 메커니즘

credibility 신뢰성, 신빙성

408 **impair** 손상[악화]시키다

unfavorable 부정적인, 호의적이 아닌; 불운한

409 **facet** 측면, 양상

innate 타고난, 선천적인 (=inborn); 고유한

empower 힘을 실어주다; 권한을 부여하다

410 **eternal** 영원한, 끊임없는

411 **attain** 얻다, 이루다

break away (from) ~로부터 벗어나다

unrestrained 제어되지 않는

412 **itinerary** 여행 일정(표)

UNIT 40 •

413 **take A into account** A를 고려하다, 계산에 넣다

in a ~ fashion ~한 방식으로

414 **flourish** 자라다, 번창하다

paradoxically 역설적으로

415 **throwaway** 쓰고 버리는 (것), 일회용(의) (=disposable)

perishable 영구적이지 않은; 망가지기 쉬운
(↔permanent 영구적인, 불변의)

out of style 유행이 지난, 구식이 된

expire 사라지다; 만기가 되다

416 **common good** 공익, 일반의 이익

driving force 원동력; 추진력

channel (생각, 감정 등을) 전하다, 돌리다; 수로(를 열다); 경로

417 **axis** 중심축

420 **vegan** 채식주의자, 비건

meditator 명상가

longevity 장수, 오래 지속됨

miserable 고생하는, 괴로운; 비참한

421 **reconstitute** 재구성하다; 원상태로 만들다

in line with ~에 따라, ~와 연결되도록

invade 침해하다; 침략하다; (손님 등이) 몰려들다

UNIT 37 부연 설명은 건너뛰어라

381 Once a bottle of perfume has been opened, it becomes susceptible to oxidation, a process that changes the chemical makeup, and therefore the smell, of the perfume.

*oxidation 산화 (작용)

QUESTION ▶ 위 문장의 밑줄 친 oxidation을 부연 설명하는 부분을 찾아 밑줄을 그으시오.

Basic Points 영어 문장에는 문장 부호(punctuation)가 매우 많이 사용된다. 콜론(:)을 제외한 일부 문장 부호 뒤 어구는 읽지 않고 건너뛰면, 문장 구조가 잘 보여서 이해가 더 쉬운 경우도 많다.

1. 콤마(,): 주로 부사구[절] 앞뒤에서 쓰이거나 어구가 나열될 때 쓰인다. 동격을 나타내어 앞의 어구를 좀 더 구체적으로 풀어서 설명하거나, 부수적인 정보를 추가로 제공한다.
2. 콜론(:): 명확하지 않은 어구를 구체적으로 설명해주므로 잘 읽는 것이 좋다. '즉'으로 해석한다.
3. 세미콜론(;): 완전한 형태의 두 절을 연결한다. 앞뒤 절의 의미 관계에 따라 적절한 접속사(그리고, 그러나, 그래서, 왜냐하면 등)로 해석한다.
4. 대시(—): (1) 콜론, 세미콜론을 대신하여 쓰인다.
   (2) 문장 중간에 나온 어구의 앞뒤에 모두 쓰이면 삽입된 정보임을 나타낸다. 동격처럼 앞에 나온 어구를 구체적으로 풀어서 설명하거나, 부수적인 정보를 추가로 제공한다.
5. 괄호( ): 위의 대시(—)와 같은 용도로 쓰인다.

382 Archaeologists have discovered the bones of ten thousand wild horses at the bottom of a cliff in France, the remains of herds stampeded over the clifftop by groups of cooperative and ingenious paleolithic hunters seventeen thousand years ago. —사관학교

*stampede (동물들이) 우르르 몰려가게 하다 **paleolithic 구석기 시대의

QUESTION ▶ 위 문장의 밑줄 친 부분이 부연 설명하는 어구를 찾아 밑줄을 그으시오.

Advanced Points 부연 설명은 보통 설명하는 어구 바로 뒤에 오지만 서로 떨어져 있는 경우도 있다. 부연 설명이 앞에 나온 어떤 어구에 대한 것인지를 문맥을 살펴서 판단하도록 한다.

383 The famous expression, "Keep your friends close, but keep your enemies even closer," was exemplified well in Nelson Mandela's attempt to learn Afrikaans, the language of his enemy. —모의

*Afrikaans 아프리칸스어 ((네덜란드어에서 발달한 언어로 남아프리카공화국에서 사용됨))

384 Geothermal heat, generated inside the Earth, helps keep the temperature of the ground at a depth of several meters at a nearly constant temperature of about 10°C to 20°C. —모의

*geothermal 지열(地熱)의

385 One factor contributes / contributing to students' difficulty in making accurate judgments of their own knowledge is hindsight bias: the tendency to assume once something happens that one knew all along that it was going to happen. −모의

*hindsight 뒤늦은 깨달음, (일이 벌어진 뒤에) 사정을 다 알게 됨

QUESTION▶ 위 문장의 네모 안에서 어법상 적절한 표현을 고르시오.

386 Based on the findings of educational psychologists, guidance on teenagers' social media usage was provided: parents should pay more attention to their children, and teachers should inform them of the negative effects.

387 Every part of history is intimately interconnected with every other part in such a way that all melt imperceptibly into one another; no part of it would be quite as it is without the preceding parts.

QUESTION▶ 위 문장에서 밑줄 친 부분의 의미로 적절한 것을 고르시오.
① All history has accumulated to create the present.
② The different histories of countries share similar characteristics.

388 Learned helplessness is based on the underlying conviction that there is no connection / separation , no matter what you do or how much you try, between your personal actions or abilities and the outcome or result — a belief that it doesn't matter what you do because it won't work anyway.

*learned helplessness ((심리)) 학습된 무기력

QUESTION▶ 위 문장의 네모 안에서 문맥에 맞는 낱말로 적절한 것을 고르시오.

389 The so-called Mozart effect — the theory that listening to Mozart will make your child smarter — is a good example of a scientific finding being distorted by the media through hype not warranted by the research. −모의

*hype 과장된 광고, 선전

390 Researchers have long observed and recorded birds building nests of different sizes and shapes (often becoming more elaborate as they matured), suggesting that there is / be some learning involved in building nests.

QUESTION▶ 위 문장의 네모 안에서 어법상 적절한 표현을 고르시오.

391 By the early nineteenth century in England, <u>traditional concepts of marriage</u> — such as an alliance between families, a pairing on the basis of wealth or birth, or an arrangement made by parents — had been changed by the romantic notion of love.

QUESTION 위 문장에서 밑줄 친 traditional concepts of marriage의 예시에 해당하는 부분을 찾아 밑줄을 그으시오.

 Main Points 앞에 나온 어구를 부연 설명하는 가장 흔한 방법은 예시를 들거나 동격구문을 이용하여 좀 더 구체적, 세부적으로 설명해주는 것이다. 하지만 부연 설명이 길고 복잡한 구조라면 이를 이해하느라 시간을 들일 필요가 없고, 앞의 내용을 이해했다면 굳이 이 부분을 읽지 않아도 될 것이다. 또한 예시가 여러 개 나열되어 있을 때도 아예 건너뛰거나 아니면 쉽게 이해되는 것만 읽고 넘어가면 된다. 즉, 부수적인 모든 것을 빠짐없이 이해하려고 하는 완벽주의를 버려야 한다.

1. 예시를 나타내는 신호어: 문장 부호 대시(—), 괄호 등과 같이 쓰이는 경우가 많다.
   for example[instance], such as, e.g., take ~ 등
   (예시 앞의 especially, particularly, in particular는 중요한 예시를 나타낸다.)

2. 동격구문의 신호어: 문장 부호 콤마(,), 세미콜론 등과 같이 쓰이는 경우가 많다.
   of[or] 뒤, that절, to-v ~, that is (to say), i.e., in other words, namely, 콤마(,)+which (is[means]) 등

392 Artists who produce fine art must be sensitive to the laws of physics. A sculpture, for example, must be stable, which requires <u>the sculptor to understand the properties of mass, weight distribution, and stress.</u>

QUESTION 위 문장에서 밑줄 친 부분의 의미로 적절한 것을 고르시오.
① applying the laws of physics to create works of art
② analyzing art works using the laws of physics

393 Many doctors are now recommending a ritual that other cultures, particularly the Swedes and Finns, have long relied on — dry-heat saunas followed by cold showers — to restore the body externally and internally.

394 Members of a group tend to avoid promoting viewpoints outside the comfort zone of consensus thinking, which may cause them to ignore individual doubts for fear of upsetting the group's balance. —모의응용

395 In Chinese food, the idea is that food should be boiling hot, because that is crucial to its flavor, embodied in the phrase "wok hei," which means the "breath" or essence of the combination of tastes added by a hot wok. —모의

*wok 웍 ((중국 요리용 냄비))

396 When a company comes out with a new product, its competitors typically go on the defensive, doing whatever they can to reduce the odds that the offering will eat into their sales. —모의

397 Being able to forgive, to let go of angry thoughts and feelings, promotes the body's natural ability to return from an aroused state to a normal state.

398 Online we can hang out in chat rooms with like-minded souls, join social networks that reflect our beliefs and interests, and even read news blogs that reflect our individual ideologies and views of the world; for instance / that is , groups are now formed less on shared activities and more on shared ideologies. —모의응용

QUESTION▶ 위 문장의 네모 안에서 문맥에 맞는 표현으로 적절한 것을 고르시오.

399 Although whales are aquatic creatures, they are mammals; in other words, they feed milk to their young and are also warm-blooded.

400 Before you give advice, that is to say, advice which you have not been asked to give, it is well to put to yourself two questions, namely, what is your motive for giving it, and what is it likely to be worth?

QUESTION▶ 위 문장에서 밑줄 친 two questions의 동격에 해당하는 부분을 찾아 밑줄을 그으시오.

401 Anxiety, which is overly zealous mental preparation for an anticipated threat, is disastrous cognitive _____ when it captures all your attention and intrudes on all other attempts to focus elsewhere. —수능응용

FILL-IN▶ ① collaboration ② interference

402 Many scientists believe that clues to much of Earth's origins, <u>as well as many other answers to life on our planet</u>, may lie within the unexplored ocean depths.

<u>QUESTION</u> ▶ 위 문장에서 밑줄 친 부분은 어느 어구에 대한 추가 정보인지 밑줄을 그으시오.

 Main Points 막연한 어구나 어려운 용어 등을 더욱 잘 이해시키기 위해 좀 더 쉬운 설명을 덧붙이는 것이 아니라, <u>또 다른 정보를 추가</u>하는 경우가 있다. 추가 정보를 나열하는 것이므로, 나열된 모든 것을 이해하려고 하지 않아도 된다.
• too, also, in addition, as well as ~, further(more), moreover
  (모두 too나 and의 의미라 할 수 있다.)

단, 아래와 같이 <u>추가되는 사항을 앞선 내용보다 더 강조하는</u> 경우는 위와 구별해서 알아두자.
• what is more, ~ as well, besides: 〈not only A but also B〉에서 B의 내용을 강조할 때의 뉘앙스로 이해한다.
• in fact, as a matter of fact, actually (사실은, 실은)

403 The total characteristics of a plant depend on which genes it has received from the parent plants, whether those genes are "switched on" (expressed), and also the interactions between the genes and environmental factors.

*express (형질을) 발현시키다

404 In convenience stores, consumers can quickly find an array of goods — bread, milk, tissues, aspirin, as well as several "efficient" self-serve items such as coffee, sandwiches, microwavable instant food, etc.

*self-serve 셀프서비스의, 직접 준비할 수 있는

405 Cost of production seems, on the surface, to be a useful element to economic analysis. Furthermore, noneconomists relate well to the concept of cost of production, while supply functions, input demand functions, and other important issues are less obvious concepts. −경찰대응용

406 A process of critique and argumentation engages all scientists. They examine things (for example, each other's ideas) and look for flaws; moreover, science has established a formal mechanism of peer review for establishing the credibility of any individual scientist's work.

*peer review 동료 평가[심사]

407 If you know how to give yourself time to rest well without worries, you can get ready to keep on working, and what is more, you can improve the quality of your work.

408 Loneliness is clearly related to impaired mental health and carries a significant social stigma as well, as the social perceptions of lonely people are generally unfavorable.

*social stigma 사회적 낙인[오명]

409 A teacher is a role model influencing every facet of the students' growth and developing their innate potentials. Besides, the teacher of today is also responsible for enabling and empowering the learner to emerge as a competent youth.

410 It goes without saying that any estimate of a modern novel is valueless unless it is based on knowledge of the great works of the past; but at the same time it is no use estimating the value of the great works of the past unless it is based on knowledge of the novels of the present. In fact, all literary work, both of the past and of today, exists as if it were in an eternal present. −경찰대응용

411 It has been claimed that no specific knowledge, or experience is required to attain insight in the problem situation. As a matter of fact, one should break away from experience and let the mind wander freely. −모의응용

SUMMARY Avoiding the existing / unrestrained knowledge helps us to find solutions.

412 Many people know that one can experience stress while traveling. However, research has found that the most common stressful travel experiences were actually related to pre-travel issues and planning, such as financial concerns, packing, making travel arrangements, and developing the itinerary.

413 Wood carving is most successful if it is in harmony with the preexisting grain and knots of the wood. _____, learning is most successful if it takes into account the preexisting behavior structures of the organism. — 사관학교

*grain (목재 등의) 결 **knot (나무의) 옹이; 마디

QUESTION 위 문장의 빈칸에 알맞은 연결어를 고르시오.
① In a similar fashion   ② On the other hand

414 When you avoid what you fear for a short time, your fear does decrease. Over a longer period, _____, avoidance allows the anxiety to flourish, paradoxically growing your fear. — 사관학교응용

QUESTION 위 문장의 빈칸에 알맞은 연결어를 고르시오.
① likewise   ② however

> **Main Points** 문장과 문장의 확실한 논리 관계를 나타내는 연결어를 보고, 뒤에 전개될 내용을 예상한 뒤 독해를 하면 이해하는 데 훨씬 도움이 된다.
> 1. similarly, likewise, in the same way, in (a) similar fashion: 서로 유사한 내용을 연결한다. 앞서 이해한 내용을 토대로 유사한 내용임을 미리 짐작하고 읽어 내려간다.
> 2. however, in contrast, on the other hand, though, nevertheless, nonetheless: 앞뒤가 서로 대조되는 내용을 연결한다. 앞서 이해한 내용을 토대로 대조되는 내용임을 미리 짐작하고 읽어 내려간다.
> *in fact, indeed: 방금 한 말에 대해 더 자세한 내용을 강조하여 덧붙이는데도 쓰이지만(← Unit 39) 반대되는 내용을 강조할 때도 쓰인다.

415 Today, products like food containers, cigarette lighters, contact lenses, and even cameras have become throwaways. Similarly, clothing and accessories are perishable / permanent in the sense that once they are out of style their usefulness expires. — 사관학교응용

QUESTION 위 문장의 네모 안에서 문맥에 맞는 낱말로 적절한 것을 고르시오.

416 Parts of human nature that seem negative can be turned to the common good, such as our tendency to imitate, which leads people to follow a leader's example. Likewise, qualities such as selfishness can be a powerful driving force if channeled correctly.

417 Most beliefs can be tested to see if they are correct or false. In the same way / However , some types of beliefs cannot be tested because we cannot get external evidence in our lifetimes (such as a belief that the Earth will stop spinning on its axis by the year 9999 or that there is life on a planet 100-million light-years away). —모의응용

QUESTION▶ 위 문장의 네모 안에서 문맥에 맞는 연결어로 적절한 것을 고르시오.

418 Unlucky people tend to be creatures of routine. In contrast, many lucky people try to introduce variety into their lives, boosting the likelihood of opportunities.

419 When a child takes an IQ test, his or her results are compared with the results of tests taken by other children of the same age. An adult's test results, on the other hand, are compared with the results of all other adults, not just adults of the same age.

420 Some people go vegan or become a meditator to get the longevity benefits of healthy habits. In fact, a healthy life is attainable for many of us with just a few small changes that aren't especially hard to do — and won't make you miserable. —경찰대응용

TOPIC▶ Great / Minor changes are enough for a healthy life.

421 To reconstitute democracy in line with our present situation, we need to challenge the frightening, but false, assumption that increased diversity automatically brings increased tension and conflict in society. Indeed, the exact reverse can be true. The reality is, conflict in society is not only necessary, it is, within limits, desirable. —사관학교응용

TOPIC▶ Diversity and conflict in a society develop / invade democracy.

GOLDEN SAYING

The pleasure we derive from doing
favors is partly in the feeling
it gives us that we are not
altogether worthless.
It is a pleasant surprise to ourselves.

-Eric Hoffer ((美 철학자))

우리가 호의를 베푸는 데서 얻는 기쁨은 부분적으로 그것(호의)이
우리에게 주는, 우리가 완전히 쓸모없지는 않다는 느낌에 있다.
그것은 우리 자신에게 즐거운 놀라움이다.

구문의 짝을 찾아라

Chapter Overview

- 짝을 이루는 구문의 앞부분에 해당되는 것이 나오면 뒤에 나올 짝을 찾아 읽어 내려간다. 그러면 문장의 구조를 좀 더 빠르고 정확하게 이해할 수 있다.

- 짝을 이루는 구문으로는 대표적인 가주어-진주어 구문 외에도 접속사, 대명사, 부사 등이 사용된 것들도 있다. 목적어 뒤에 특정한 전명구를 동반하는 동사도 이에 해당된다고 볼 수 있다.

Chapter Goals

1 짝을 이루는 구문들의 종류를 나열할 수 있다.

2 특정 동사를 보고 목적어 뒤에서 짝을 이루는 전명구를 문장에서 찾을 수 있다.

Must-know Words & Lexical Phrases

U N I T 4 1 •

422 desirable 바람직한, 호감 가는

alter 바꾸다; 변하다

enhance (질, 능력 등을) 강화하다, 높이다

trait 특성

424 exceptionally 매우, 유난히; 예외적으로

425 nurture 키우다; 양육하다

426 negotiation 협상

cf. negotiator 협상가

427 doubtful 불확실한; 의심스러운

cf. doubt 의심(하다)

undoubtedly 확실히, 의심할 여지 없이

428 magnify 과장하다; 크게 하다, 확대하다

429 imaginary 가상의, 상상에만 존재하는

cf. imaginative 상상력이 풍부한, 창의적인

430 organized 조직화된; 정리된; 유기적인

celestial 천체의, 하늘의

phenomenon ((복수형 phenomena)) 현상

431 uneasy 불편한; (마음이) 불안한

credit for ~에 대한 공로[인정]

432 look upon[on] A as B A를 B로 여기다

U N I T 4 2 •

433 disapproval 반대; 비난; 못마땅함 (↔approval 찬성; 승인)

deterrent 제지, 억제

434 somehow 어떻게든

435 give off (열, 빛 등을) 방출하다[내다]

core 핵심적인, 아주 중요한

finite 한정된, 유한한 (↔infinite 무한한)

depletion 고갈, 소모

436 in A's presence A의 앞에서, 면전에서

conscious 의식하는

(↔unconscious 무의식적인)

437 want ((주로 복수형)) 욕구; 결핍, 부족

439 avid 열렬한, 열심인; 열망하는 (=keen)

　spring up (갑자기) 나타나다, 생겨나다

　following 추종자[팬]들; 다음의, 다음에 계속되는

440 yield (수익, 결과 등을) 낳다, 가져오다

　full measure of 충분한, 완전한

　(↔short measure of 모자라는, 부족한)

　substance 내용, 요지; 물질; 실체, 본질

　afford 제공하다; (금전적, 시간적) 여유가 되다

　cf. **affordable** (가격이) 알맞은, 감당할 수 있는

　degenerate 전락하다; 악화되다; 타락한 (사람)

　superficial 깊이 없는, 피상적인

　exclusive 배타적인; 독점적인, 전용의

　mutual 상호적인

441 give way to A A로 바뀌다; A에 못 이기다

　pendulum (시계의) 추, 진자

442 relay (정보 등을 받아서) 전달하다

UNIT43 •

443 adversity 역경, 불운

　cf. **adverse** 부정적인, 불리한; 반대의

　deed 행동, 실행

444 superior 뛰어난, 우월한; 윗사람, 상급자

　(↔inferior 열등한; 아랫사람, 하급자)

　cf. **superiority** 우월성

　appreciate 인정하다; 평가하다; 감사해하다

445 ongoing 계속 하고 있는, 진행 중인

　inborn 타고난, 선천적인

447 inseparable 불가분의, 떼어놓을 수 없는 (↔separable 분리 가능한)

448 status quo 현재의 상황

449 vital 필수적인, 매우 중요한; 생명의, 생명 유지와 관련된

　sector 부문, 분야

450 severity 심각(함), 격렬(함)

　cf. **severe** 심각한; 엄한

intensity 강도; 강렬함

　cf. **intense** 극심한, 강렬한

451 unconventional 독특한 (↔conventional 평범한; 전통적인)

UNIT44 •

453 abuse 함부로 사용하다, 남용하다; 남용, 오용; 학대(하다)

　commodity (유용한) 것; 상품, 물품; 원자재

454 attribution (성질 따위가) 있다고 생각함, 귀속; 속성

　likable 호감이 가는, 마음에 드는

455 temptation 유혹

　in terms of ~의 관점에서

456 hold back (from v-ing) (v하기를) 망설이다

　give A a shot A를 시도해 보다

457 rush through ~을 서둘러 다루다[처리하다]

　engage with ~에 관여하다

458 malfunction 기능부전, 고장; 제대로 작동하지 않다

　massive 대규모의, 거대한; 심각한

459 map out (세심히) ~을 계획[준비]하다

460 take root 뿌리를 내리다, 널리 받아들여지다

　validity 타당성; (법적으로) 유효함

　cf. **valid** 타당한, 근거 있는; 유효한

461 dare to-v v할 엄두를 내다, 과감히[감히] v하다

462 particle 아주 작은 조각[입자]; 극소량

　digestive 소화의

　enzyme 효소

　act on ~에 작용하다; ~에 따라 행동하다, 조치를 취하다

　raw material 원료, 재료; 원자재

it ~ to-v[that]

422 Is it socially desirable or acceptable to change certain genes of a normal human individual to alter or enhance traits?

> **QUESTION** 위 문장에서 진주어 부분을 찾아 밑줄을 그으시오.

423 The invention of the microscope made it possible for scientists to learn more about what causes diseases.

> **QUESTION** 위 문장에서 진목적어 부분을 찾아 밑줄을 그으시오.

424 More than any other development, it has been the exceptionally rapid growth of computer technology that has changed every aspect of our lives.

> **QUESTION** 위 문장에서 강조되고 있는 부분을 찾아 밑줄을 그으시오.

🌱 **Main Points** 어떤 어구가 오면 그것과 짝을 이루는 다른 어구가 뒤에 이어질 것이 예상되는 구문이 있다. 대표적으로는 가주어 it ~ to-v[v-ing, that, whether 등], 가목적어 it ~ to-v[v-ing, that], 강조구문의 it is ~ that[who, which]이 있다. 이외에 아래와 같은 구문도 같이 알아두자.
- It takes 시간 to-v: v하는 데 얼마의 시간이 걸리다
- It costs 비용 to-v: v하는 데 얼마의 비용이 들다

🌱 **For Reading Speed** 주어 자리에 it이 보이는데 앞에 나온 어구를 가리키는 대명사가 아니라면 가주어나 강조구문의 it으로 예상하고 뒤에 나올 to-v[that] 등을 찾아 읽어 내려간다.

---

425 It is careful planning, not luck, which results in chances to nurture a new or unique idea that takes you to the next level in your life.

> **QUESTION** 위 문장에서 밑줄 친 It is와 짝을 이루는 어구를 찾아 밑줄을 그으시오.

✳ **Advanced Points** 구문과 짝을 이룰 가능성이 있는 것이 뒤에 두 개 이상 있는 문장은 문맥을 파악해서 해당되는 구문과 짝이 되는 부분을 찾아야 한다.

---

426 It goes without saying that preparation is the key to any negotiation and it is no surprise to find that the most successful negotiators are more prepared than unsuccessful negotiators.

427 It is true that intelligent students would undoubtedly score high in memory functions, but it is doubtful whether they are also fluent in producing creative ideas.

428 Every man who knows how to read has it in his power to magnify himself, to multiply the ways in which he exists, to make his life full, significant, and interesting. —Aldous Huxley ((英 작가))

429 Though some people have felt that only the lonely play with imaginary playmates, the research makes it very evident that it is often the highly superior and imaginative child who invents these creatures. —수능응용

430 It was patterns in the organized and regular motions of stars and other celestial objects that ancient humans tried to recognize, just as present-day scientists search for patterns and trends in natural phenomena. —모의응용

431 What is it that makes us uneasy about accepting credit for something wonderful we have done? We feel proud of our accomplishments and our skills, but we don't know how to take credit for them gracefully.

432 Thomas Edison was looked upon as a fool by his teachers, and it was only because his mother inspired him to believe that one day he would do something great that he became the man he was.

> **QUESTION** 위 문장의 내용과 일치하는 것을 고르시오.
> ① Edison achieved his accomplishments because his mother made him believe in himself.
> ② Edison's teacher played him for a fool after Edison believed he would do something great.

Plus⁺ 가목적어를 갖는 관용 표현

- take **it** for granted that ~   ~을 당연한 것으로 여기다
- see (to **it**) that ~   반드시 ~하도록 하다, ~하도록 조치하다
- have **it** that ~   ~라고 말하다, ~라고 주장하다
- take **it** that ~   ~라고 추정하다, ~라고 여기다

짝을 이루는 접속사

---

433 In small villages, everyone, in a sense, becomes a judge; in such societies, social disapproval of people's activities can serve <u>both</u> as powerful punishment for and as strong deterrent to crime. −경찰대

QUESTION 위 문장에서 밑줄 친 <u>both</u>와 짝을 이루는 접속사를 찾아 밑줄을 그으시오.

✎ **Main Points** 둘 이상의 어구가 짝을 이루어 접속사 역할을 하는 경우도 잘 알아두자. 병렬구조를 이루는 접속사(◁ Unit 25)를 포함해서 아래와 같은 것들이 있다.

- both A and B   A와 B 둘 다
- neither A nor B   A도 B도 아닌
- not only[just, merely, simply] A but (also) B   A뿐만 아니라 B도 (= B as well as A)

- either A or B   A와 B 둘 중 하나
- not A but B   A가 아니라 B (= B but not A)

- so+형용사[부사](+a/an+명사)+that   아주 ~해서 …하다; …할 정도로 한
- such(+a/an)(+형용사)+명사+that   아주 ~해서 …하다; …할 정도로 한
- no sooner ~ than ...   ~하자마자 …하다 (= hardly[scarcely] ~ when[before] ..., as soon as)
- (just) as ~, so ...   (꼭) ~인 것처럼 …하다

✎ **For Reading Speed** 짝을 이루는 첫 번째 어구가 보이면 뒤에 나올 두 번째 어구를 찾아 읽어 내려가도록 한다.

---

434 When two people communicate or work together, only one of two possibilities will result: either the more negative person will lower the spirits of the more positive person, or the more positive person will somehow lift the spirits of the other. −EBS 응용

---

435 Not only batteries are / are batteries at risk of giving off toxic gases if damaged, but core ingredients such as lithium and cobalt are finite and extraction can lead to water pollution and depletion among other environmental consequences. −경찰대응용

QUESTION 위 문장의 네모 안에서 어법상 적절한 표현을 고르시오.

---

436 Children should never be "required" to learn the name of anything in their study of nature, but the name should be used so often and so naturally in their presence that they will learn it without being conscious of the process.

−모의응용

TOPIC the necessity of conscious / unconscious learning for children

437 Human beings have unlimited wants, and resources available in nature, which should be used to meet those human wants, are limited. That is, there is never such a complete time that a human being is satisfied / disappointed and not in need of anything.

QUESTION 위 문장의 네모 안에서 문맥에 맞는 낱말로 적절한 것을 고르시오.

438 No sooner had we learned a new idea or technique than another one came along and replaced or enhanced what we had learned.

439 Scarcely had Arthur Conan Doyle begun publishing Sherlock Holmes stories when an avid fan base sprang up — the beginning of an international following.

440 As reading without discussion can fail to yield the full measure of understanding that should be sought, so discussion without the substance that good and great books afford is likely to degenerate into little more than an exchange of superficial opinions. −경찰대

SUMMARY Reading and discussion are in exclusive / mutual relation.

441 Just as there has never been a day that did not give way to night or a storm that lasted forever, so we move back and forth on the pendulum of life — the day and the night, the good and the bad, etc.

442 Just as you cannot explain a thought to someone if you did not fully understand that thought, neither can you translate or interpret something without mastery of the subject matter being relayed.

443 Every society needs heroes, and every society has them. <u>Some heroes</u> shine in the face of great adversity, performing amazing deeds in difficult situations; others do their work quietly, unnoticed by most of us, but making a difference in the lives of other people. ―수능

QUESTION 위 문장에서 밑줄 친 Some heroes와 짝을 이루는 대명사를 찾아 밑줄을 그으시오.

444 Geniuses are <u>too</u> much superior to those around them to be understood at once; and their books, music, statues, or pictures are usually <u>too</u> superior to be quickly appreciated.

QUESTION 위 문장에서 밑줄 친 too와 짝을 이루는 어구를 각각 찾아 밑줄을 그으시오.

✎ **Main Points** 둘 이상의 어구가 짝을 이루는 대명사, 부사구, 전명구 등도 잘 알아두자. 쉬워 보이지만 문장이 길고 복잡해지면 자칫 놓치게 되는 경우가 많으므로 주의해야 한다.

- some ~ others ...   어떤 것[사람]은 ~, 다른 것[사람]은 ...
- one ~ the other ...   (둘 중) 한쪽은 ~, 다른 한쪽은 ...
- the former ~ the latter...   전자는 ~, 후자는 ...
- the one ~, the other ...   전자는[후자는] ~, 후자는[전자는] ...
- too ~ to-v   너무 ~해서 v할 수 없는, v하기에는 너무 ~한
- ~ enough to-v   v할 (수 있을) 만큼 ~한, v하기에 충분히 ~한
- so ~ as to-v   v할 만큼 ~한, (매우) ~해서 v하다
- between A and B   A와 B 사이에
- from A to B   A에서 B까지

이 외에도 v-ing, to-v 등 특정 준동사를 이끄는 동사들도 기억해두는 것이 좋다.
- spend+시간[돈]+(in) v-ing: v하는 데 시간[돈]을 쓰다
- have difficulty[trouble, a hard time] (in) v-ing: v하는 데 어려움을 겪다

✎ **For Reading Speed** 첫 번째 어구가 보이면 두 번째 어구가 나오리라 예상하고 이를 찾아 읽어 내려가는 것이 좋다.

445 There is an ongoing debate in the field of emotional intelligence: some scholars see emotional intelligence as a set of skills that can be taught and learned, while others say it is largely inborn.

446 The important difference between technology and magic is not that technology works and magic does not, but that one deals with what we understand, while another / the other with what still remains a mystery.

QUESTION 위 문장의 네모 안에서 어법상 적절한 표현을 고르시오.

447 There is an inseparable relation between diligence and success. The former is the cause and the latter is the effect.

448 When setting goals, it is recommended that the goals be difficult enough to be a challenge, yet realistic enough to achieve. The key is to balance the gap between the status quo and the goal.

449 Volunteers are so vital a part of the nation's economy, social atmosphere, and overall well-being, as to relieve a huge burden from the public sector and create a cooperative atmosphere in the community. −사관학교응용

450 Some physicians propose that there is no direct relationship between the severity of the wound and the intensity of pain, but that the meaning our minds give to an injury greatly determines the level of pain. −모의응용

451 In a tour of over 10 different galleries and art spaces, the visitors will see everything from new and unconventional street art to classic pieces of art displayed in the local museum.

452 I wish I hadn't spent so much energy when I was younger trying to please those whose opinions never mattered.

453 We abuse land because we regard it _____ a commodity belonging to us. When we see land _____ a community to which we belong, we may begin to use it with love and respect. – Aldo Leopold ((美 작가))

QUESTION ▶ 위 문장의 빈칸에 공통으로 들어갈 전치사를 쓰시오.

🖋 **Main Points** 목적어 다음에 전명구를 동반하는 다음의 동사들은 관용적 표현으로 익혀두어야 한다.

• regard[look upon, think of, view, see] A **as** B	A를 B로 여기다
• blame[scold, thank] A **for** B	A를 B의 이유로 비난하다[꾸짖다, 감사하다]
• substitute A **for** B	A로 B를 대신하다 (= replace B with A)
• prevent[stop, keep, discourage] A **from** B(v-ing)	A가 B하지 못하게 하다
• distinguish[tell, know] A **from** B	A를 B와 구별하다
• extract A **from** B	A를 B에서 뽑아내다
• rob[deprive] A **of** B	A에게서 B를 빼앗다
• remind[inform, convince] A **of** B	A에게 B를 상기시키다[알리다, 확신시키다]
• owe[attribute, ascribe] A **to** B	A를 B의 탓[덕택]으로 돌리다
• prefer A **to** B	B보다 A를 선호하다
• limit A **to** B	A를 B로 제한[한정]하다
• provide[supply, present] A **with** B	A에게 B를 공급하다 (= provide B for A)

위의 동사들이 보이면 동반하는 전명구를 찾아 읽어 내려가도록 한다.

454 Perfection, or the attribution of that quality _____ celebrities, creates a perceived distance that the general public cannot relate to — making those who never make mistakes perceived as being less attractive or likable. – 모의응용

QUESTION ▶ 위 문장의 빈칸에 들어갈 전치사를 쓰시오.

✳ **Advanced Points** 위 문장은 〈attribute A to B〉 구문이 〈attribution of A to B〉로 변환된 것이다. 즉 〈타동사의 명사형 +of A+전명구〉의 형태가 되는 것들도 잘 알아두자.

• substitution of A for B	• prevention of A from B
• discouragement of A from B	• extraction of A from B
• attribution of A to B	• preference of A to B

455 Even though it has become fashionable to view the differences between men's and women's minds as social in origin, the temptation to seek an explanation in terms of inborn differences between the sexes remains strong.

456 Keep your self-doubt and fear of failure from holding you back from giving your dreams a shot by pushing yourself to take action.

457 Rushing through a lot of complex content robs most students in class of the time they need to engage deeply with the novel ideas, leaving little chance of recall.

TOPIC the positive / negative effects of speedy learning

458 Deprived of oxygen, the body's cells malfunction and die; deprived of information, the organization's individuals and departments cannot work properly. To avoid malfunction and massive failure in the organization, it's important to keep communicating.

459 You can map out your goals and tape them to the refrigerator so you're reminded of both what you want to accomplish and how you're getting there.

460 Ultimately in science, new ideas will take root only if you can convince your colleagues of the validity of your results.

461 Too often we limit our employment opportunities to what we're familiar with and we do not dare to think about trying training in a completely new field.

462 Chewing leads to smaller particles for swallowing, and more exposed surface area for digestive enzymes to act on. In other words, it means the extraction of more fuel and raw materials from a mouthful of food. -모의

GOLDEN SAYING

We pay a price when we deprive
children of the exposure
to the values, principles,
and education they need
to make them good citizens.

-Sandra Day O'Connor ((美 대법관))

우리는 아이들을 좋은 시민으로 만들기 위해 필요한 가치, 원칙,
그리고 교육을 접하는 것을 빼앗아 갈 때 대가를 치른다.

길고 복잡한 문장의 해결

Chapter Overview

- 실제로 독해에서 접하는 문장은 관계사절이 한 문장에 두 개 이상 들어가 있거나, 관계사절 내에 관계사절이 겹쳐 들어가 있는 경우가 드물지 않다. 이 경우 문장의 선행사와 관계사절의 범위를 올바로 파악하는 것이 중요하다.

- 길고 복잡한 문장에 비교구문이나 특수구문이 포함되면 해석의 어려움이 배가 된다. 각 구문의 특성에 따라 대처법을 알아보고, 긴 문장에 적용해본다.

Chapter Goals

1 길고 복잡한 문장에서 관계사절을 [ ]로 묶고 선행사를 찾을 수 있다.

2 길고 복잡한 문장에서 비교구문을 이루는 표현을 알아보고 해석할 수 있다.

3 특수구문의 특성에 따라 주목해야 할 요소를 알고 문장의 구조를 파악할 수 있다.

4 긴 문장을 의미 단위별로 끊고 문장의 핵심 내용을 파악할 수 있다.

Must-know
Words &
Lexical
Phrases

UNIT 45 •

464 **transport** 데려가다, 이동시키다; 수송, 운반

465 **consist of** ~로 구성되다 (=be comprised of)

   cf. consist in ~에 있다, 존재하다

   geometric 기하학의, 기하학적인

   figure 도형; 형태; 수치; 인물; 계산하다

467 **immerse** 몰입하다, 열중하다; 담그다

468 **school** 학파; 학부; (해양 동물의) 떼, 무리

   relief (고통 등의) 완화, 경감; 안도, 안심

   alleviate (고통을) 완화하다 (=ease)

   sympathetic 동정 어린, 동정적인; 동조하는, 공감하는

   cf. sympathy 동정, 연민; 동의, 공감

   distress 괴로움, 고통; 곤경; 괴롭히다

470 **systematically** 조직적으로, 체계적으로

   confront 직면하다, 맞서다

   contradiction 모순; 반박, 부정

   cf. contradict 모순되다; 반박하다

   overvalue 과대평가하다 (↔undervalue 과소평가하다)

   disregard 무시하다 (=ignore)

   refute 반박[논박]하다; 부인하다

471 **entity** 존재, 실재(하는 것)

472 **socialite** 사교계 명사

UNIT 46 •

473 **justify** 정당화하다, 옳다고 하다; 해명하다

474 **collectively** 총체적으로; 모두 합쳐서; 집합적으로

   cf. collective 집단적인; 공동의; 집단(의), 공동체

475 **sidetrack** (하던 일에서) 곁길로 새게 하다; 탈선, 이탈

   chore 하기 싫은[따분한] 일; (정기적인) 일

476 **likelihood** (어떤 일이 있을) 가능성

477 **bounce back** 회복하다 (=recover)

480 **pile up** 쌓다, 축적하다

   detection 발견; 발각

   cf. detect 발견하다, 감지하다 (=discover)

principle 원리, 원칙; 주의

⚠ **principal** 주요한, 주된; (단체의) 장

dissimilar 다른, 같지 않은 (↔similar 비슷한)

abnormal 이례적인, 변칙의; 비정상적인 (↔normal 보통의)

481 **poetic** 시적인; 시의

mythological 신화적인, 신화의

cf. **mythology** 신화; 근거 없는 믿음

482 **outstanding** 눈에 띄는, 두드러진; 뛰어난

associate 동료, 친구; 연관 짓다; 제휴하다

UNIT **47** •

483 **draw on** ~에 의지하다; ~을 이용하다

faith 믿음; 신념

inevitably 반드시, 필연적으로

cf. **inevitable** 피할 수 없는, 필연적인

485 **imperative** 필수적인 (=vital); 긴급한; 명령하는, 단호한; ((문법)) 명령문의

486 **engage in** ~에 종사하다; ~에 참여하다, 관여하다

487 **humanity** 인류; 인간성

superstition 미신

conviction 확신; 신념; 유죄 선고

488 **obesity** 비만

texture 식감; 질감, 구조, 조직

489 **downside** 부정적인[불리한] 면; 하강; 아래쪽(의)

unethical 비윤리적인 (↔ethical 윤리적인)

490 **tremendous** 엄청난, 대단한

innermost 가장 깊숙한

491 **privileged** 특권을 가진

entail 수반하다

492 **diverting** 흥미로운, 재미있는, 즐거운

cf. **divert** 방향을 바꾸게 하다; 즐겁게 해주다

call up 상기시키다

utterly 완전히, 순전히 (=totally)

distinct 다른, 별개의; 뚜렷한, 분명한

spiritual 정신적인; 종교적인

UNIT **48** •

493 **demanding** 힘든, 부담이 큰; 요구가 많은

inspiring 고무적인, 영감을 주는; 용기를 주는

494 **assess** 평가하다

extraction 추출, 뽑아냄, 얻어냄

proportion 비율; 부분

upfront 선행 투자의; 솔직한

495 **terminology** 전문 용어

neutral 중립적인; 중립(국가)

496 **label A as B** A를 B라고 (꼬리표를 붙여) 분류하다

subjective 주관적인 (↔objective 객관적인)

of little[no] account 중요하지 않은

497 **fruitful** 유익한, 생산적인

archive 기록 보관소

extensive 방대한, 넓은

498 **render** 표현하다; (어떤 상태가 되게) 만들다

spatial 공간적인, 공간의

configuration 배치, 배열

499 **take aback** 당황하게 하다, 깜짝 놀라게 하다

elaborate 정교한, 정성을 들인

500 **encompass** 포함하다

corporate 기업의; 공동의

관계사절이 여러 개 들어간 복잡한 문장

463 One thing I know is that the only ones among you who will be really happy are those who will have sought and found how to serve. – Albert Schweitzer ((슈바이처))

QUESTION ▶ 위 문장에서 관계사절을 모두 찾아 [ ]로 묶은 뒤, 각 관계사절의 선행사에 밑줄을 그으시오.

🖋 **Main Points** 한 문장에 관계사절이 여러 개 있을 경우 Unit 07, 11에서 학습한 것처럼 관계사절을 [ ]로 묶고 수식 대상인 선행사를 파악하면 문장의 기본 구조가 더 잘 보인다. 관계사절을 이끄는 목적격 관계대명사는 종종 생략되며 관계부사도 일반적 선행사와 쓰이면 자주 생략된다. 이때 관계사절은 〈S′+V′ ~〉의 형태가 된다. (◁ Unit 19)

464 Music can transport you to that wonderful holiday, that perfect relationship, that great night out, or anytime when you were in a situation where you enjoyed yourself.

QUESTION ▶ 위 문장에서 관계사절을 모두 찾아 [ ]로 묶은 뒤, 각 관계사절의 선행사에 밑줄을 그으시오.

✳ **Advanced Points** 관계사절을 [ ]로 묶다 보면, 관계사절 속에 또 다른 관계사절이 겹쳐 있을 수도 있다.

명사 [관계사절1~~명사~~[관계사절2]]

각 관계사절의 범위와 수식 대상인 선행사를 잘 파악하여 [ ]로 묶어야 한다.

465 When I entered the museum, the first thing that caught my eye was a colorful painting consisting of traditional patterns, which were illustrated with geometric figures.

466 You can get away from envy by enjoying the pleasures that come your way, by doing the work that you have to do, and by avoiding comparisons with those whom you imagine, perhaps quite falsely, to be more fortunate than yourself. – Bertrand Russell ((英 철학자))

467 Unless an actor speaks and moves in the manner in which the imaginary character whose part he or she is playing would do, it will be hard for the audience to feel immersed in the story. – 모의응용

468 One school of modern economic theory argues that people give to charities in part because of the pleasure they get either from imagining the relief of those they benefit or from their own relief from alleviating their sympathetic distress. *－모의응용*

TOPIC▸ understanding why people donate to / benefit from charities

469 Our modern society should provide appropriate education or training sessions for a sufficient number of people who possess the technical skill required to maintain and develop the numerous devices upon which our convenience depends.

470 Confirmation bias is a term for how the mind systematically avoids confronting contradiction by overvaluing evidence that confirms what we already think or feel and undervaluing or simply disregarding evidence that refutes it. *－수능응용*

QUESTION▸ 위 문장에서 밑줄 친 Confirmation bias의 예로 적절한 것을 고르시오.
① 가짜 뉴스가 영향력을 갖는 현상　② 무신론자가 종교적 깨달음을 얻는 것

471 The phrase "emotional labor" refers to a situation where work-related entities regulate the way a person manages his or her emotions in order to shape the state of mind of another individual, such as a customer.

472 "Yellow journalism" sometimes took the form of gossip about public figures, as well as about socialites who considered themselves private figures, and even about those who were not part of high society but had found themselves involved in a scandal, crime, or tragedy that journalists thought would sell papers. *－모의*

473 If all mankind minus one were of one opinion, and only one person were of the contrary opinion, mankind could be no more justified in silencing that one person, than he, if he had the power, would be justified in silencing mankind. –John Stuart Mill ((英 철학자))

QUESTION 위 문장이 뜻하는 바로 적절한 것을 고르시오.
① 반대하는 한 사람을 침묵시키는 것은 정당화될 수 없다.
② 반대하는 한 사람이 있으면 나머지는 침묵해야 한다.

Main Points 복잡한 문장에 비교구문까지 결합하면 독해의 부담을 더욱 가중시킨다. 비교구문을 이루는 표현들은 문장 안에서 서로 떨어져 있기 마련이므로, 우선 그것들에 네모 상자를 씌운 후 의미를 정확히 파악하자.

474 How interested people are in their work, how much control they feel they have over their work, and how much support they get from their employer are collectively much more important in predicting job satisfaction than are their salaries.

475 Generally speaking, the more uncertain of success or easily sidetracked you are, the more likely it is that you will do an assignment or chore later. –모의응용

476 In reality, the people who are most different from us probably have the most to teach us. The more we surround ourselves with people who are the same as we are, who hold the same views, and who share the same values, the greater the likelihood that we will shrink as human beings rather than grow. –수능응용

477 It's not the failures nor wrong decisions that define us so much as how we respond to our life challenges, growing to become better people, and learning to bounce back.

478 In conversation, one is likely to find out certain things about another person, not so much from what that other person says as from how he or she says it, for the speaker cannot avoid giving the listener clues about where they come from or what sort of people they are.

QUESTION 위 문장이 뜻하는 바로 적절한 것을 고르시오.
① The contents and method of conversation represent the speaker.
② Not the contents but the way someone talks conveys who he or she is.

479 The great use of school education is not so much to teach you lots of different pieces of knowledge as to teach you the art of learning, so you can apply that art for yourself to any matter you will face in later life.

480 Science consists not in the collection of varied facts any more than the random piling up of stones is architecture — but in the detection of the principles which relate even the most dissimilar and abnormal facts to each other and of the order which combines the parts into a whole.

481 No single flower is so universally known, so closely connected with the culture of many civilizations, and so rich in poetic and mythological significance as the rose.

TOPIC The rose is the most [insignificant / meaningful] flower in the world.

482 Changes in employment may bring advantages in many ways. Yet they also come with some disadvantages, the most outstanding of which is the fact that one is never as efficient in a new position, a new environment, and among new associates, as he is where he is familiar with the details of his work and has the confidence of his associates. —사관학교응용

SUMMARY A job change causes employees to be [less efficient / more skillful] at the new workplace.

483 It is when you are going through your most difficult experiences that you must draw on your ability to control your mind and have faith that the difficulty you face is simply part of the process that will inevitably bring you through to your goal.

QUESTION 위 문장에서 강조되고 있는 부분을 찾아 밑줄을 그으시오.

 Main Points 복잡한 문장에 여러 특수구문이 결합되면 아래와 같이 구조를 파악한다.
1. 강조구문의 it is와 that(또는 who(m), which)에 네모 상자를 씌운 후, 강조되는 부분을 확인한다.
2. 도치구문은 주어와 동사를 찾아 표시한다.
3. 삽입어구는 ( )로 묶고 나머지로 문장 구조를 판단한다.
4. 동격구문은 =로 연결한다.
5. 공통구문은 특정 어구(X)에 공통으로 연결되는, 즉 병렬구조를 이루는 어구(A, B)를 확인한다.
   AX+BX ⇒ (A+B)X   XA+XB ⇒ X(A+B)

484 Such has been the effect of materialism that it tends to be believed by many, rather uncritically, that wealth is a central life goal and that the possession of it will increase our happiness.

*materialism 물질(만능)주의

485 It is so simple to find time to be out of your home, whether for a walk, for a run, or just for a phone call you take on a park bench, and it is imperative, no matter how briefly, for us to get sunlight.

486 Anybody who has been seriously engaged in scientific work of any kind realizes that over the entrance to the gates of the temple of science are written the words: YOU MUST HAVE FAITH. −Max Planck ((독일 물리학자))

487 Humanity's growing freedom from superstition results from the conviction that the world is not governed by caprice, but that it is a world of order and can be understood if we will only try hard enough and be smart enough.

*caprice 변덕, 갑작스러움

488 There is good evidence that the current obesity crisis is caused, in part, not by what we eat (though this is of course vital, too) but by the degree to which our food has been processed before we eat it, because processed soft texture of food is an important factor in weight gain. –모의응용

489 The avocado is a pear-shaped green-fleshed fruit and is known for its health benefits, but for some, the fact that there are downsides to the avocado due to its recent trade explosion — massive water usage, or the potential for unethical treatment of workers in certain production areas — might be a concern.

490 It was a tremendous moral shock to most intelligent people that the proof of man's having uncovered one of the innermost secrets of the universe should have been the making and using of a weapon of mass destruction, the atomic bomb.

491 Nineteenth-century hermeneuticians challenged the assumption that the author had any privileged insight into the meaning of his or her text by critically examining the active process entailed in reading, and thus the need to construct rather than merely to recover meaning from a text. –모의응용

*hermeneutician (성경 또는 고전의) 해석학자

492 However poetic, realistic, impressive, or diverting an object is, it is not an object of art unless it calls up in a man the feeling, utterly distinct from all other feelings, of joy, of spiritual union with another (the author) and with others (listeners or spectators) who perceive the same artistic work.

UNIT 48
50단어 내외의 긴 기출 문장

493 One of the most demanding and, at the same time, inspiring aspects of translating for children is the potential for such creativity that arises from what a literary critic has called the 'childness' of children's texts: 'the quality of being a child — dynamic, imaginative, experimental, interactive and unstable.' –모의응용

QUESTION 위 문장에서 동사를 찾아 밑줄을 그으시오.

Main Points 수능의 경우 한 문장에 30단어가 넘어가는 것이 드물지 않고, 때로는 50단어 내외의 긴 문장이 등장하기도 한다. 시험에서 유독 길고 복잡한 문장이 등장했을 때 당황하지 않고 지금까지 학습한 사항들을 적절히 적용하면, 시간을 많이 허비하지 않고도 핵심을 파악해낼 수 있을 것이다.

특히 다음과 같은 구문이 포함되면서 문장이 길어지는 경우가 많다.
1. 예시의 나열: 앞서 학습했듯이 전부 다 읽으려 하지 말고 쉽게 이해되는 것만 파악하고, 건너뛴다.
2. 수식어구 및 삽입구[절]: ( )로 묶고 남은 어구에서 문장의 핵심인 주어와 동사를 먼저 파악한 후, 목적어나 보어 등의 의미를 덧붙여 나간다. 각 어구의 의미 단위를 파악하며 문장을 이해해 본다.

494 The energy output from solar panels or wind power engines, where most investment happens before they begin producing, may need to be assessed differently when compared to most fossil fuel extraction technologies, where a large proportion of the energy output comes much sooner, and a larger (relative) proportion of inputs is applied during the extraction process, and not upfront. –수능응용

495 According to many sociologists, the study of what our society calls 'art' can only really progress if we drop the highly specific and ideologically loaded terminology of 'art', 'artworks' and 'artists', and replace these with the more neutral and less historically specific terms 'cultural forms', 'cultural products' and 'cultural producers.' –모의

496 The consequence of scientism is that non-scientific approaches to reality — including all the arts, religion, and personal, emotional, and value-laden ways of encountering the world — may become labeled as merely subjective, and therefore of little _____ in terms of describing the way the world is.

-수능응용

*scientism 과학만능주의 **value-laden 가치 판단적인; 개인적 의견에 영향을 받는

FILL-IN ① account　② controversy

497 A journey through the stacks of a real library has the possibility to be more fruitful than a trip through today's distributed virtual archives, because it seems difficult to use the available "search engines" to emulate efficiently the mixture of predictable and surprising discoveries that typically result from a physical shelf-search of an extensive library collection. -수능응용　　*emulate 따라 하다

498 Since photographs did such an excellent job of representing things as they existed in the world, painters were freed to look inward and represent things as they were in their imagination, rendering emotion in the color, volume, line, and spatial configurations native to the painter's art. -수능

499 So slow and painful is the process of mastering a technique, whether of handcraftsmanship or art, so imbued are we with the need of education for the acquirement of knowledge, that we are taken aback by the realization that all around us are creatures carrying on the most elaborate technique, going through the most complicated procedures and possessed of the surest knowledge without the possibility of teaching. -사관학교응용

*handcraftsmanship 수공예가의 손재주 **imbue (사상, 감정 등을) 고취하다, ~에게 불어넣다

500 Investigations into the economics of information encompass a variety of categories, including the costs of information and its services; the effects of information on decision making; the savings from effective information acquisition; the effects of information on productivity; and the effects of specific agencies (such as corporate, technical, or medical libraries) on the productivity of organizations. -수능

천일문 완성 문제집 MASTER
Training Book

Training Book

500 SENTENCES
MASTER

천일문 완성
문제집

Practice Makes Perfect!

실력은 하루아침에 이루어지지 않죠.
노력만이 완벽을 만듭니다.
〈천일문 완성 문제집 Training Book〉은
〈천일문 완성〉의 별책 문제집으로
〈천일문 완성〉과 동일한 순서로 구성되어 있어
학습 내용을 편하게 확인하고 적용해볼 수 있습니다.
완성편 학습과 병행하세요.

| 별도 판매 | 정가 13,000원

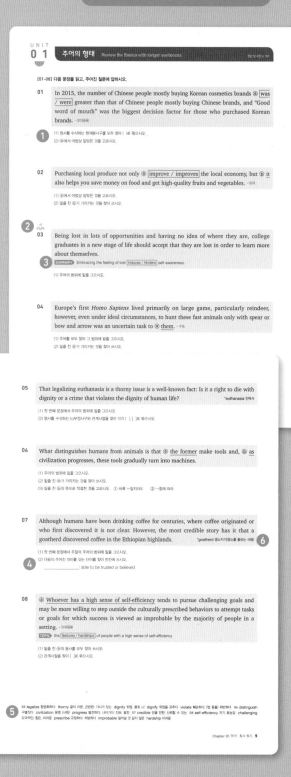

1 학습한 구문을 적용시키는 문제
2 고난도 문항 표시
3 TOPIC·SUMMARY·FILL-IN으로 문장의 핵심 파악 테스트
4 추가 주요 구문 문제로 복습
5 문제 풀이에 걸림돌이 되지 않도록 보기 편한 위치에 어휘 제시
6 학습 범위를 벗어나는 고난도 어휘는 별도 제시

1 구문 이해 확인에 특화된 다양한 문제

04 Europe's first *Homo Sapiens* lived primarily on large
however, even under ideal circumstances, to hunt these f
bow and arrow was an uncertain task to ⓐ them. ―수능

(1) 주어를 모두 찾아 그 범위에 밑줄 그으시오.
(2) 밑줄 친 ⓐ가 가리키는 것을 찾아 쓰시오.

04 ⓐ <u>Many</u> who have experienced a major loss often go on
spite of their hardships, because they focus on wha
circumstance ⓑ <u>rather than</u> on what they have lost. ―모의

(1) 밑줄 친 ⓐ를 수식하는 부분을 [ ]로 묶으시오.
(2) 밑줄 친 ⓑ로 연결되어 병렬을 이루는 어구를 찾아 각각 밑줄을 그으시오.

2 TOPIC·SUMMARY·FILL-IN 문제

08 ⓐ Whoever has a high sense of self-efficiency tends to p
may be more willing to step outside the culturally prescrib
or goals for which success is viewed as improbable by
setting. ―모의응용

TOPIC the features / hardships of people with a high sense of self-efficiency

03 Being lost in lots of opportunities and having no idea
graduates in a new stage of life should accept that they a
about themselves.

SUMMARY Embracing the feeling of lost induces / hinders self-awareness.

(1) 주어의 범위에 밑줄 그으시오.

01 According to research, what separates innovators from
"_____": the ability to successfully connect seem
problems, or ideas from different fields. ―모의응용

FILL-IN ① prioritizing   ② associating

(1) 주어의 범위에 밑줄 그으시오.
(2) 명사를 수식하는 to부정사구의 범위를 ( )로 묶으시오.

3 추가 주요 구문 적용 문제

05 That legalizing euthanasia is a thorny issue is a well-know
dignity or a crime that violates the dignity of human life?

(1) 첫 번째 문장에서 주어의 범위에 밑줄 그으시오.
(2) 명사를 수식하는 to부정사구와 관계사절을 찾아 각각 ( ), [ ]로 묶으시오.

What distinguishes humans from animals is that ⓐ <u>the former</u>
civilization progresses, these tools gradually turn into machines.

(1) 주어의 범위에 밑줄 그으시오.
(2) 밑줄 친 ⓐ가 가리키는 것을 찾아 쓰시오.
(3) 밑줄 친 ⓑ의 뜻으로 적절한 것을 고르시오. ① 비록 ~일지라도   ② ~함에 따라

4 어법 문제

02 For innovation to be less challenging, the link conne
community, the producer and the user, should be tighter,
rapid feedback ⓐ is / are a source of good ideas.

(1) 주절의 동사를 찾아 쓰시오.
(2) ⓐ에서 어법상 알맞은 것을 고르시오.

Modern biology is as important as it is inspiring, with exciting break
ⓐ changing / changed our very society; biology has even entered
investigations, with terms such as DNA fingerprinting now ⓑ (be) pa
vocabulary.

(1) ⓐ에서 어법상 알맞은 것을 고르시오.
(2) ⓑ에서 주어진 단어를 어법상 알맞은 형태로 쓰시오.
(3) 다음의 주어진 의미를 갖는 단어를 찾아 빈칸에 쓰시오.
_____ : a discovery or achievement that comes after a lot of hard work

5 주요 내용 이해와 관련된 문제 (밑줄 친 단어 의미/해석/어휘 영영 정의 등)

05 ⓐ <u>Throughout the last two decades many developing countries</u>
tourism market as part of globalization processes, but these cou
negative public and media image which made ⓑ <u>it</u> challenging
over tourists with countries with strong and familiar brands. ―모

TOPIC the difficulty of developing countries in losing / taking the initiative in the global t

(1) 밑줄 친 ⓐ에서 주어와 동사를 찾아 쓰시오.
(2) 밑줄 친 ⓑ가 가리키는 것을 찾아 밑줄 그으시오.
(3) 밑줄 친 ⓒ가 가리키는 것을 찾아 쓰시오.

07 Although humans have been drinking coffee for centuries
who first discovered it is not clear. However, the most
goatherd discovered coffee in the Ethiopian highlands.

(1) 첫 번째 문장에서 주절의 주어의 범위에 밑줄 그으시오.
(2) 다음의 주어진 의미를 갖는 단어를 찾아 빈칸에 쓰시오.
_____ : able to be trusted or believed

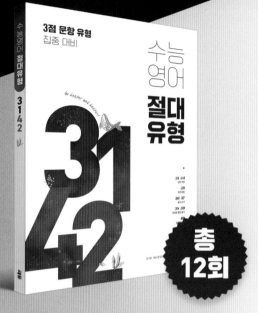

① 구문   판매 1위 '천일문' 콘텐츠를 활용하여 정확하고 다양한 구문 학습

끊어읽기   해석하기   문장 구조 분석   해설·해석 제공   단어 스크램블링   영작하기

② 문법·서술형   쎄듀의 모든 문법 문항을 활용하여 내신까지 해결하는 정교한 문법 유형 제공

객관식과 주관식의 결합   문법 포인트별 학습   보기를 활용한 집합 문항   내신대비 서술형   어법+서술형 문제

③ 어휘   초·중·고·공무원까지 방대한 어휘량을 제공하며 오프라인 TEST 인쇄도 가능

영단어 카드 학습   단어 ↔ 뜻 유형   예문 활용 유형   단어 매칭 게임

④ 선생님 보유 문항 이용

Online Test   OMR Test

cafe.naver.com/cedulearnteacher

쎄듀런 학습 정보가 궁금하다면?

쎄듀런 Cafe

· 쎄듀런 사용법 안내 & 학습법 공유
· 공지 및 문의사항 QA
· 할인 쿠폰 증정 등 이벤트 진행

대한민국 영어 구문의 바이블!

천일문
New Edition
시리즈

개정에 도움을 준 선생님들께서

마음을 담아, 추천사를 남겨주셨습니다.

전에도 이미 완벽했었지만, 거기에서 더 고민하여 선정한 문장의 선택과 배치는 가장 효율적인 학습환경을 제공합니다. 양질의 문장을 얼마나 많이 접해봤는지는 영어 학습에서 가장 중요한 요소 중 하나이며, 그 문장들을 찾아다니며 시간을 낭비할 필요 없이 천일문 한 권으로 해결하시기 바랍니다.

김명열 | 대치명인학원

굳이 개정하지 않아도 좋은 교재이지만 늘 노력하는 쎄듀의 모습답게 더 알찬 내용을 담았네요. 아이들에게 십여 년이 넘는 시간 동안 영어를 가르치면서도 영어의 본질은 무시한 채 어법에만 치우친 수업을 하던 제게 천일문은 새로운 이정표가 되어주었습니다. 빨라진 시대의 흐름에 따라가지 못하는 한국의 영어교육에 조금이라도 이 책이 도움이 될 것 같아 기대감이 큽니다.

김지나 | 킴스영어

독해는 되지만 글에서 의미하는 바를 찾지 못하고 결국 내용을 어림짐작하여 '감'으로 풀게 되는 학생들에게는 더더욱 필요한 능력이 문해력입니다. '감'으로 푸는 영어가 아닌 '문해력'에 기초하여 문제를 풀기 위한 첫 번째 단계는 정확한 문장 구조분석과 정확한 해석입니다. 많은 학생들이 천일문 시리즈를 통해 1등급 성취의 열쇠를 손에 넣을 수 있기를 바랍니다.

박고은 | 스테듀입시학원

책의 가장 큰 장점은 수험생을 위해 단계별로 정리가 되어 있다는 점입니다. 고3으로 갈수록 추상적인 문장이 많아지며 읽고 문장을 바로 이해하는 능력을 키우는 것이 중요한데, '천일문 완성'의 경우 특히 추상적 문장을 많이 포함하고 있어, 문장을 읽으면서 해당 문장이 무슨 내용을 나타내는지, 포함한 글이 어떤 내용으로 전개될 것인지 유추하면서 읽는다면 수험생들에게 큰 도움이 되리라 생각합니다.

이민지 | 세종 마스터영어학원

수능 및 모의평가에서 자주 출제되는 핵심 구문들을 챕터별로 정리할 수 있어서 체계적입니다. 이 교재는 막연한 영어 구문 학습을 구체화해 배치해두었기 때문에, 학습자 입장에서는 등장할 가능성이 큰 문형들을 범주화하여 학습할 수 있습니다. 저 또한 학생 때 천일문 교재로 공부했지만 지금 다시 봐도 감동은 여전합니다.

안상현 | 수원시 권선구

천일문 교재가 처음 출간되었을 때 이 책으로 영어 구문 수업을 하는 것은 교사로서 모험이었습니다. 선생님 설명이 필요 없을 정도로 완벽한 교재였기 때문입니다. 영원히 현재진행형인 천일문 교재로 영어 읽는 법을 제대로 반복 학습한다면 모든 학생들은 영어가 주력 과목이 될 수 있을 겁니다.

조시후 | SI어학원

영문법 학습의 올바른 시작과 완성은 문법이 제대로 표현된 문장을 통해서만 얻어질 수 있다고 생각합니다. 심혈을 기울여 엄선한 문장으로 각 문법의 실제 쓰임새를 정확히 보여주는 천일문은 마치 어두운 동굴을 비추는 밝은 햇불과 같습니다. 만약 제가 다시 학생으로 돌아간다면, 주저하지 않고 선택할 첫 번째 교재입니다. '학습에는 왕도가 없다'라는 말이 있지요. 천일문은 그럴싸해 보이는 왕도나 허울만 좋은 지름길 대신, 멀리 돌아가지 않는 바른길을 제시합니다. 영어를 영어답게 접근하는 방법, 바로 천일문에 해답이 있습니다.

황성현 | 서문여자고등학교

변화하는 시대의 학습 트렌드에 맞춘 고급 문장들과 정성스러운 해설서 천일비급, 빵빵한 부가 학습자료들로 더욱 업그레이드되어 돌아온, 천일문 개정판의 출시를 진심으로 축하드립니다. 전체 구성뿐만 아니라 구문별로 꼼꼼하게 선별된 문장 하나하나에서 최고의 교재를 만들기 위한 연구진들의 고민 흔적이 보입니다. 내신과 수능, 공시 등 어떤 시험을 준비하더라도 흔들리지 않을 탄탄한 구문 실력을 갖추길 원하는 학습자들에게 이 교재를 강력히 추천합니다.

김지연 | 송도탑영어학원

그동안 천일문과 함께 한지도 어느새 10년이 훌쩍 넘었습니다. 천일문은 학생들의 영어교육 커리큘럼에 필수 교재로 자리매김하였고, 항상 1,000문장이 끝나면 학생들과 함께 자축 파티를 하던 때가 생각납니다. 그리고 특히 이번 천일문은 개정 작업에 참여하게 되어 개인적으로 더욱 의미가 있습니다. 교육 현장의 의견을 적극적으로 반영하고 참신한 구성과 문장으로 새롭게 변신한 천일문은 대한민국 영어교육의 한 획을 그을 교재가 될 것이라 확신합니다.

황승휘 | 에버스쿨 영어학원

문법을 자신의 것으로 만드는 방법은 어렵지 않습니다. 좋은 교재로 반복하고 연습하면 어제와 내일의 영어성적은 달라져 있을 겁니다. 저에게 진짜 좋은 책 한 권, 100권의 문법책보다 더 강력한 천일문 완성과 함께 서술형에도 강한 영어 실력자가 되길 바랍니다.

민승규 | 민승규영어학원

저는 본래 모험을 두려워하는 성향입니다. 하지만 제가 전공인 해운업계를 떠나서 영어교육에 뛰어드는 결정을 내릴 수 있었던 것은 바로 이 문장 덕분입니다.

"Life is a journey, not a guided tour." 인생은 여정이다, 안내를 받는 관광이 아니라.
- 천일문 기본편 461번 문장

이제 전 확실히 알고 있습니다. 천일문은 영어 실력만 올려주는 책이 아니라, 영어라는 도구를 넘어 수많은 지혜와 통찰을 안겨주는 책이라는 것을요. 10대 시절 영어를 싫어하던 제가 내신과 수능 영어를 모두 1등급 받을 수 있었던 것, 20대 중반 유학 경험이 없는 제가 항해사로서 오대양을 누비며 외국 해운회사를 상대로 온갖 의사전달을 할 수 있었던 것, 20대 후반 인생에 고난이 찾아온 시기 깊은 절망감을 딛고 재기할 수 있었던 것, 30대 초반 온갖 도전을 헤치며 힘차게 학원을 운영해 나가고 있는 것 모두 천일문에서 배운 것들 덕분입니다. 이 책을 학습하시는 모든 분들이, 저처럼 천일문의 막강한 위력을 경험하시면 좋겠습니다.

한재혁 | 현수학영어학원

최고의 문장과 완벽한 구성의 "본 교재"와 학생들의 자기주도 학습을 돕는 "천일비급"은 기본! 학습한 것을 꼼꼼히 점검할 수 있게 구성된 여러 단계(해석, 영작, 어법 수정, 문장구조 파악 등)의 연습문제까지! 대한민국 최고의 구문교재가 또 한 번 업그레이드를 했네요! "모든 영어 구문 학습은 천일문으로 통한다!" 라는 말을 다시 한번 실감하게 되네요! 메타인지를 통한 완벽한 학습! 새로운 천일문과 함께 하십시오.

이헌승 | 스탠다드학원

"천일문"은 단지 수능과 내신 영어를 위한 교재가 아니라, 언어의 기준이 되는 올바른 영어의 틀을 형성하고, 의미 단위의 구문들을 어떻게 다루면 좋을지를 스스로 배워 볼 수 있도록 해주는 교재라고 생각합니다. 단순히 독해를 위한 구문 및 어휘를 배우는 것 이상으로, (어디로나 뻗어나갈 수 있는) 탄탄한 기본기를 형성을 위한 매일 훈련용 문장으로 이보다 더 좋은 시리즈가 있을까요. 학생들이 어떤 목표를 정하고 그곳으로 가고자 할 때, 이 천일문 교재를 통해 탄탄하게 형성된 영어의 기반이 그 길을 더욱 수월하게 열어줄 것이라고 꼭 믿습니다.

박혜진 | 박혜진영어연구소

최근 학습에 있어 가장 핫한 키워드는 문해력이 아닌가 싶습니다. 영어 문해력을 기르기 위한 기본은 구문 분석이라 생각합니다. 다년간 천일문의 모든 버전을 가르쳐본 결과 기초가 부족한 학생들, 구문 학습이 잘 되어 있는데 심화 학습을 원하는 학생들 모두에게 적격인 교재입니다. 천일문 교재를 통한 영어 문장 구문 학습은 문장 단위에서 시작하여 더 나아가 글을 분석적으로 읽을 수 있어 영어 문해력에 도움이 되어 자신 있게 추천합니다.

아이린 | 광주광역시 서구

고등 내신에도, 수능에도 가장 기본은 정확하고 빠른 문장 파악! 문법 구조에 따라 달라지는 문장의 의미를 어려움 없이 이해할 수 있게 도와주는 구문 독해서! 추천합니다!

안미영 | 스카이플러스학원

쎄듀 초·중등 커리큘럼

	예비초	초1	초2	초3	초4	초5	초6
구문		신간 천일문 365 일력 |초1-3| 교육부 지정 초등 필수 영어 문장		초등코치 천일문 SENTENCE 1001개 통문장 암기로 완성하는 초등 영어의 기초			
문법					초등코치 천일문 GRAMMAR 1001개 예문으로 배우는 초등 영문법		
			신간 왓츠 Grammar		Start (초등 기초 영문법) / Plus (초등 영문법 마무리)		
독해				신간 왓츠 리딩 70 / 80 / 90 / 100 A / B 쉽고 재미있게 완성되는 영어 독해력			
어휘				초등코치 천일문 VOCA&STORY 1001개의 초등 필수 어휘와 짧은 스토리			
		패턴으로 말하는 초등 필수 영단어 1 / 2 문장 패턴으로 완성하는 초등 필수 영단어					
ELT	Oh! My PHONICS 1 / 2 / 3 / 4 유·초등학생을 위한 첫 영어 파닉스						
	Oh! My SPEAKING 1 / 2 / 3 / 4 / 5 / 6 핵심 문장 패턴으로 더욱 쉬운 영어 말하기						
	Oh! My GRAMMAR 1 / 2 / 3 쓰기로 완성하는 첫 초등 영문법						

	예비중	중1	중2	중3
구문	신간 천일문 STARTER 1 / 2			중등 필수 구문 & 문법 총정리
문법	천일문 GRAMMAR LEVEL 1 / 2 / 3			예문 중심 문법 기본서
	GRAMMAR Q Starter 1, 2 / Intermediate 1, 2 / Advanced 1, 2			학기별 문법 기본서
	잘 풀리는 영문법 1 / 2 / 3			문제 중심 문법 적용서
	GRAMMAR PIC 1 / 2 / 3 / 4			이해가 쉬운 도식화된 문법서
			1센치 영문법	1권으로 핵심 문법 정리
문법+어법	첫단추 BASIC 문법·어법편 1 / 2			문법·어법의 기초
문법+쓰기	EGU 영단어&품사 / 문장 형식 / 동사 써먹기 / 문법 써먹기 / 구문 써먹기			서술형 기초 세우기와 문법 다지기
				올쏨 1 기본 문장 PATTERN 내신 서술형 기본 문장 학습
쓰기	거침없이 Writing LEVEL 1 / 2 / 3			중등 교과서 내신 기출 서술형
		개정 중학 영어 쓰작 1 / 2 / 3		중등 교과서 패턴 드릴 서술형
어휘	신간 천일문 VOCA 중등 스타트/필수/마스터			2800개 중등 3개년 필수 어휘
		어휘끝 중학 필수편 중학 필수어휘 1000개	어휘끝 중학 마스터편 고난도 중학어휘 +고등기초 어휘 1000개	
독해	Reading Relay Starter 1, 2 / Challenger 1, 2 / Master 1, 2			타교과 연계 배경 지식 독해
	READING Q Starter 1, 2 / Intermediate 1, 2 / Advanced 1, 2			예측/추론/요약 사고력 독해
독해전략			리딩 플랫폼 1 / 2 / 3	논픽션 지문 독해
독해유형			Reading 16 LEVEL 1 / 2 / 3	수능 유형 맛보기 + 내신 대비
			첫단추 BASIC 독해편 1 / 2	수능 유형 독해 입문
듣기	Listening Q 유형편 / 1 / 2 / 3			유형별 듣기 전략 및 실전 대비
		쎄듀 빠르게 중학영어듣기 모의고사 1 / 2 / 3		교육청 듣기평가 대비